"Never take the gift of time for granted. For you can do much with your life when you master your own 5x5 you will thrive. Do as much good as you can in this life"
- R!k Schnabel

5x5 TO THRIVE
GET MORE MONEY + JOY IN CHANGING TIMES

R!K SCHNABEL
THE BRAIN UNTRAINER

#1 International best-selling author of "ROAR! Courage – From Fear to Fearless, A Richer Way To Think" "7 Beliefs That Will Change Your Life" and "The Life Coach Millionaires."
www.LifeBeyondLimits.com.au

Get your **FREE ticket** to learn from R!k Schnabel in his *Life Coach + NLP Practitioner* introduction training, valued at $597 by using this link:
https://lifebeyondlimits.com.au/free-nlp-training

5x5 TO THRIVE

5x5 To Thrive Copyright © 2022 R!k Schnabel and Life Beyond Limits Pty Ltd. R!k Schnabel has asserted his right to be identified as the author of this Work in accordance with the Copyright, Designs and Patents Act 1988

All rights reserved. No part of this book may be used or reproduced by any means, graphic, electronic, or mechanical, including photocopying, recording, taping or by any information storage retrieval system without the written permission of the author except in the case of brief quotations embodied in critical articles and reviews.

First published in 2022 by Life Beyond Limits Pty Ltd

P.O. Box 772, Merimbula New South Wales Australia 2548

Life Beyond Limits is a part of Life Beyond Limits group of companies and can be found at lifebeyondlimits.com.au

Because of the dynamic nature of the Internet, any web addresses or links contained in this book may have changed since publication and may no longer be valid. To locate any web addresses, it is best to use the search function via www.lifebeyondlimits.com.au.

The author of this book does not dispense medical advice or prescribe the use of techniques as a form of treatment for physical, emotional, psychological or medical problems without the advice of a physician, either directly or indirectly. The intent of the author is only to offer information of a general nature to help you in your quest for emotional and spiritual well-being. In the event you use any of the information in this book for yourself, which is your constitutional right, the author and the publisher assume no responsibility for your actions.

Any people depicted in stock imagery provided by Thinkstock are models, and such images are being used for illustrative purposes only. Certain stock imagery © Thinkstock.

5x5 To Thrive is a systemised way to improve your productivity. Discover how to get more done, make more money and deliver more joy to your life.

Want to master your time? Use your *5x5 To Thrive* within 'Triple 8 Time' to bring order to chaos. Plus harness your 'Key Drivers' within your 'Power Time' and you become unstoppable. If you think this book gives you more than an improvement in throughput, you're right. It's much more.

5x5 To Thrive is a paradigm shift. It gives you new ways to think about your time that will have you increase your value, and then your productivity - and so your income.

Since Covid-19, times have changed and so the rules for business and life have changed too.

Never has there been a period of time in this century when being productive is more valued and more important than now.

Though time will move on without you if you do not use it.

5x5 To Thrive is not a mere time management book. It's how to give back to you. Glean tips on how to get more joy from your life and gain some timely money-building tips.

The value of your time changes when you change how you measure time. Time increases when you adjust your purpose of time and the moment you stop playing indoctrinated mind games with time.

There are many myths about time that distract the multitudes from believing they don't have enough time or worse, enough money to set themselves free.

5x5 To Thrive is a book that will shift your paradigm of time and liberate you — for good.

Contents

Contents		5
Introduction		7
1.	The World Conditions A Weak Mind	12
2.	Your Diary Time Saver	23
3.	Time: Your Only Limited Resource	31
4.	How Do You Measure Your Time?	35
5.	A Career or Calling?	43
6.	More Value Equals More Time	52
7.	What's Your Power Time?	59
8.	Your Time First	69
9.	Bending Time	80
10.	Is Time An Illusion?	87
11.	Turn Distraction To Action	102
12.	Systemise To Save Time	108
13.	Mind Games We Play With Time	117
14.	Use Your Triple 8 Time	134
15.	The Biggest Time Vampire Of All	139
16.	Twenty-Five Time Wasters	146
17.	Twenty Time Savers	157

18.	*5x5 To Thrive* Gets You Productive	170
19.	Your *5x5 To Thrive* Perfect Practice	177
20.	Time To Ask Better Questions	184
21.	Guard Your Time From Thieves	194
Closing Thoughts		203
About The Author		205
When You Untrain Your Brain		207
Other Books By The Author		212
Life Coach + NLP Practitioner Training		216
Bibliography		222

Introduction

The first thing I would like you to get from the outset is how much I care about time. Using my time with proficiency has helped me to achieve success in my careers in record time. It has helped me to defy statistics and take a start-up venture into the black, in its first year of operation.

By the end of this book, I hope that you will care as much for time as I do. Afterall, time is all you have and what you do with it will determine the quality of your life.

Though due to Covid-19, inflation, climate change and shifting financial markets, times have changed. Faster and more than ever before. We are living in uncertain times and only one thing is certain—more change is coming.

Readers of the Gnostics or followers of Nostradamus or astrologer Jessica Adams will attest, there is imminent change still to come. If they are right, we haven't seen anything like what is to come. A life that we have taken for granted will be no longer. We will all need to change, and the first step is to make time your friend, not a stranger.

Adjust too your sails for what is most likely a changing of the guard as the United States of America discovers that they are no longer united. There may well be a shift in the world's superpowers. As predicted by American billionaire investor, Ray Dalio. Dalio said, "When there is a shift of power, the falling power rarely falls with grace."

I am not here to scare you. I'm here to prepare you. You have time to shift. You have time to shuffle and to change. But don't sit on your hands for too long, if at all.

Negative emotions are your greatest deficit, time is greatest asset and consciousness is the goal.

What you hold, not in the palm of your hand, but in the lap of your future is time. Your greatest asset is time, and in these changing times, you need to plan your time more than ever before.

You have probably felt this time coming, somewhere deep in your soul. Particularly if you're intuitive or empathic. If you have, you will also know that negative emotions are your greatest deficit, time is your greatest asset and consciousness is the goal. I'll explain in great detail how you can improve how you think about time and use it wisely.

Miguel de Cervantes said, "Forewarned, forearmed; to be prepared is half the victory." Though this *victory* I speak of is the victory of reclaiming five key areas of your life:
1. Reclaim your health.
2. Reclaim your mind.
3. Reclaim your finances.
4. Reclaim your soul and your vehicle to achieve all of this is possible with the final element.
5. Reclaim your time.

Are you saying I've lost some of these things? As you read, you will quickly discover that the answer to that question is 'YES!' Yes, you have most likely lost your control of all five. Though like cashing in any good reality check, you will have to walk up to a mirror and be honest with yourself to see it, and then accept it.

**Time is your friend. Though don't be a stranger to it and let it pass by. You either use it or lose it.
Time moves with or without you.**

As a transformational coach and brain untrainer, I can tell you here and now, that a transformation cannot happen without first accepting reality and a plan to change.

My intention is to focus you. I want to wake you up if you are not awake already—while you have time.

Instead of calling this book '5x5 To Thrive,' I almost called it '5x5 To Survive.' Though I felt the title had a too sombre tone to it. Irrespective, I want to be real with you, though understand that there is much you can do to help yourself in these changing times. Again, the key is your time and not watching it pass by, but taking some necessary steps to protect yourself, your friends, and your family for what is to come.

Time is your friend. Though don't be a stranger to it and let it pass by. You either use it or lose it. Time moves with or without you.

So how can you use it to the best of your ability?

Time only asks three questions. These questions help it to know if it is honoured and respected. Those three questions?

What will you do?
How will you do it? And…
When will you start?

Don't waste too much time thinking about these questions. It's time to make some important decisions about your life and your future.

The moment you know *what* you are doing, and you are proficient in *how* you are doing it. You are clear *when* to start doing it, you advance your worth higher up the ladder of humanity's food chain. You are no longer fodder, at the beckoned call, at the whim of others. Your life becomes your own. If you haven't yet caught on, I'm talking about freedom. Freedom from too many systems to mention here right now that are enslaving you.

I haven't spoken out about this too much on social media, because when I do, I'm shut down. Believe me when I say that there are many people who do not want you to reclaim those *five key areas of your life*.

Freedom is never given; it must be earned. To gain it, it takes conscious effort on your part and unwavering commitment. Freedom is the ultimate gift. It is one of life's true treasures. It is a privilege for those who respect their time. Though to earn it, you must learn to claim back your time.

Claiming back your time, means you will no longer wait in line for whatever is left; the dregs left behind by controllers of our time. You will have cut the shackles of the rulers who wish for you to obey their whims and serve them until your final breath. These people will no longer be your concern. You will no longer be beholden to them; you will be free. Truly free to live your purpose or your destiny.

You may be thinking that I'm speaking of people who control you and your time. I am. But I will not speak of them again until later in this book, as we are a mere few pages in. I promise though that there are people aiming to steal your time and claim your life.

Make no mistake. Respecting, valuing, and honouring your time is to honour your unique purpose. Yes, I truly do believe we are all here for a reason. Perhaps you have found yours and you now honour your soul's mission. Because without doing so, time will pass you by in the blink of an eye. It reminds me of a story.

Finally, before we dig in. Thank you for purchasing this book. It means a lot to me. Because my aim is to help the world wake up from their time myths and poor illusions. My aim is to help you to get more done in a day and live a life beyond limits—without excuses.

Happier times are ahead for those who plan.

R!k Schnabel

1. The World Conditions A Weak Mind

It was December 1982. At the time, I was the assistant to the Advertising Manager. It was my first serious job. I was about to turn 21 when Doug Frazer, my boss, asked me, "It's your 21st birthday party this weekend isn't it?" I nodded, a little reflectively because I'd never had a birthday party before. I didn't know who to be or how to respond really. He cocked his head at my limited response and continued, "Are you looking forward to it?"

I don't know what it was exactly. Perhaps it was knowing that I was officially about to become an adult? Maybe it was the fact that I could legally vote. It could have been that I felt

the swell of being considered a man was all too confusing for me.

If we've never met before, there's a little back story that you need to know. I was a poor kid of immigrant parents who were both were unfortunately born in Germany in the thick of World War II.

When I was born, growing up in a Germanic household in Altona East, Victoria Australia, I quickly learned that my mother couldn't tolerate too much noise at the dinner table. Perhaps due to having to hunker down in her cellar, nestling my brother, while bombs fell around her. A whipping cane stood in the corner of our kitchen menacingly.

My dad, well that's another story. He was born into an orphanage and any self-esteem was beaten out of him by the nuns. All he wanted was peace after experiencing the nuns and, death and bloodshed that he saw in arctic Winters fighting the Russians. He became a prisoner of war in a Russian prisoner-of-war camp and was one of fifty or so men who survived. He lived off a quarter of a potato a day. He was valued, because he helped his Russian captors rebuild the P.O.W. camp after a bombing raid.

I had no story. I was a nothing from the Western Suburbs of Melbourne. I had no looks. I wasn't especially strong or brilliantly athletic. I wasn't smart or even charismatic. I was however the best drawer in all my classes, but art wasn't valued at all back then. Instead, I was bullied and called 'stupid,' and I believed them.

I didn't know what it meant to grow your self-esteem back then. None of us did. The schoolyard was held together by an unspoken primitive law where strength and speed were the currency.

If I had anything to gloat about at all, I was about to become a man. While I had no idea of what that meant or who I had to be, I was truly excited about the prospect of turning 21.

Doug wasn't overweight, he was thickly set and for his age, he was still strong as an ox. He had a presence that demanded respect. I saw men younger, stronger and older than him that somehow feared him. He who was to be obeyed, with his grey and white goatee and thick black rimmed glasses sat opposite me as we carefully checked and improved the copy of a store catalogue. Prior to printing store catalogues, you know the ones you get in your mailbox. Doug and I had to make sure all the copy describing every article was 100% correct—and especially the prices or heads would roll.

Doug Frazer reminded me of actor Leo McKern. Remember *Rumpole of the Bailey*? Our whole advertising team agreed. Though one association he made clear for us never to make, was a distinction between Frazer and Fraser. He was not to be confused with our then Prime Minister Malcolm Fraser, the leader of the Liberal Party of Australia. Doug was more right wing than left. I thought he was a liberal man, but he loathed Fraser. It may have been due to Fraser's part in enforcing the conscription of Australian troops to the Vietnam War however, I think it had more to do with Frasers conniving and dirty politics that he played to attain the leadership.

Doug controlled the airwaves on our department radio and when parliament sat, we had to listen. This explains why I am so appalled at our leaders who acted like school yard thugs. Shouting at one another, name calling until an appalling crescendo of rants ensued until the Speaker, the Legislative Assembly's 'independent and impartial representative' would yell "Order. Order!"

He loved his politics and had a quick wit. Though I had to improve my articulation and choice of words. He prepared me for my Neuro Linguistic Programming (NLP) training. He picked me up on every word chose that was inaccurate or poorly chosen. Articulation and word choice mattered to Doug. Conversing with him at times was like a harrowing journey with a lumberjack, willing to cut down your sentences with majestic precision. Our early days were stressful for a Westie, filled with slang, gleaned from the rough end of town.

Time is a gift.
It's a gift that you are given at birth along with free will.

I looked down at the catalogue's colour proofs, proof-reading the copy. Spellchecking every word, following each and every line as Doug's razer focus eyes checked the original typed words on A4 sheets of paper. It had to be right.

Back then, I was a clean-shaven lad with my rebellious locks of long shoulder length hair. I surfed. I played electric guitar in band. I drank, smoked and loved rock and roll, and I looked the part. Doug, well, he didn't like me at all. At first anyway. Doug hated that John Clark, the General Manager hired me, instead of him. Though over time we became friends, and he became the father I never had. He became my Mister Miyagi, my mentor and sage. He warmed to me, and I stopped being frightened of him. Yet, I was always respectful.

Doug could clearly see my excitement. Then he did what he usually did when he got serious. He lowered his glasses, peered over the top of them and said, "Don't wish your life away." "Huh?" I replied, to which he retorted, "I think you mean 'excuse me?'" He continued, "After 21 your life speeds up. Before you know it, you will wake up to an alarm you should not have set. Because today your work life is over. You are retired."

He was right. Life after 21 seemed to speed up. Every year got faster and faster as I got older.

The world conditions a weak mind.
It will take advantage of your naïve soul if you let it.

Doug was 63 years old then, and on retirement, he would hand over his senior role to me. At 24 I accepted his role as Advertising Manager and hoped that I had learned enough from him to take over the helm of his ship. Although tiring from childish behaviour of our leaders in parliament and preferring other childish rockers I steered the atmosphere of our office into another direction. I changed the radio dial from parliament to 3XY, the latest rock and pop station. A station I enjoyed my first stint as a DJ at 16 years old. For one hour at least.

Three years after my 21st, at 66 years old Doug retired and died only a few years later. That job was everything to Doug and like many, without purpose, without will, we die.

Here I am today, writing this at 61. Just two years younger than Doug was back then. He was right. Time has passed so quickly.

I thought that after 21 I would be free. Free of other people's rules and conditions. Free of a world that told you what to do. How naïve I was.

As I got older, I discovered that the world conditions a weak mind. It will take advantage of your naïve soul if you let it. So, your life's mission is to strengthen your character and recondition your mind or face being conditioned to be someone's servant. You have the time to strengthen your mind—if you choose to.

We must claim back our minds. We must demand the return of our futures. We must be ever present, ever conscious of our time and what we can do with this gift in this lifetime.

It took me forty years before I realised that if we are going to be free and do anything that is good in this world, we must awaken. Awaken to our unconscious saboteur and the stream of beliefs and ideals that are not our own. Ideas that somehow landed as truths in our minds. Truths that came from our parent's voices that rung in our ears for most of our lives. Worse, truths through the exposure of the incessant advertising, the media and the moguls behind darkened, impenetrable walls.

I spent 20 years in advertising. I know how clever the specialists are at conditioning us. Let alone those that pay their agencies handsomely to condition the masses.

Every industry is clawing their way to the top of the pyramid, like a bucket of crabs to gain a percentage or two of market share. And they will create any plausible lie to gain that foothold. For many, a one percent increase in market share can mean an extra one hundred million dollars. These industries will steal your time if you let them.

The sugar industry, the wheat industry, the meat industry, the pharmaceutical industry, the car industry the oil industry, the banking industry to name a few… I don't need to go on. I'm sure you get the idea. The more ignorant we are of the clandestine meetings that happen behind closed doors, the more easily we become entrained, indoctrinated, and lead astray.

Ironically, the mediums that the moguls use to distract us, are also the same mediums that hold the power to inform us. Yet the latter is rare. Though we must be awake enough to discern between fiction and fact. Fiction will steal your time and it may take you a lifetime to find your way back on track. So, we must sort the distractions, the divisive, maligned messages and propaganda from the useful pieces of information that help us, not hinder us. While social media, TV and the press, and the internet are the preferred tools of distraction. We can find refuge among the plethora of books, talks, trainings and the mentoring meetings and coaching sessions hold the power to awaken us. The message is simple. Wake up. Wake up. Wake up.

It's a *Matrix* blue pill or red pill moment.

We must claim back our minds. We must demand the return of our futures. We must be ever present, ever conscious of our time and come to know what we can do with our gifts, in this lifetime.

Time is your gift. It's a gift that you are given at birth along with your free will. You can use it wisely. You can use it to live your dreams or to learn something of value in this life. But I implore you not to fear life or fritter away your time. Worse, do not make excuses for not living out your life fully; purposefully. Our distractions, excuses and justifications will do that.

If you are serious about boosting your time and monetary position, this book has arrived at the perfect time for you.

Two of the most common excuses that limit people's lives are a lack of *time* and *money*. If you are using these excuses, they will hold you down, keep you stuck and leave you playing small for the rest of your life. They will weaken your mind and worse, your will.

Sadly, these excuses slip out of people's mouths all too easily and way too often. Particularly when opportunities come knocking at your door.

You will know how they sound. "I don't have enough time" some will say. Yet, we at birth, are granted a lifetime. "But I don't have the money" is a typical second line of defence. Though proven strategies can deliver you all the money you need. Though you must be courageous and conscious to shift gears and shift your mindset.

Time and money excuses derive from our fears. The fear of success or worse, failure. The fear of change. The fear of appearing foolish. The fear of fear itself.

When you whole-heartedly believe that you don't have enough time or money, your situation turns hopeless. You become helpless to a myth. This believable myth solidifies a low self-esteem and sends a terrible signal to our brains. Our head, heart and gut brains. These thoughts can only have our confidence plummeting towards the gutter.

Any reference to anyone in this book has been concealed to protect their identity.

In writing this book, I specifically researched and designed it to help you to remove those two excuses from your life. As you read, you will start to feel your mindset shift. Your productivity will improve as I share proven strategies to add value to your time and so your financial situation I hope too will improve.

I will even share new paradigms of how to think about your time and money, that for me have altered my life in magnificent ways. Purposeful ways.

If you are serious about boosting your time and monetary position, then this book has arrived at the perfect time for you. But it may require some new whole-hearted decisions for you to become a person of value.

I will explain how our conditioning and associated neurology will at times let us down and how you can remedy that.

I'll even give you real life examples, mostly from my coaching work. Though please understand that all my coaching work I use here is for your benefit. Though my clients' names are strictly confidential.

I have worked with some big names and at times celebrities who insist on 100% confidentiality. They allow me to use their case histories for teaching purposes, but I'm never to reveal their identities. Therefore, any reference to anyone in this book has been concealed to protect their identity. I have changed their names and details to protect the identity of all my clients. I'm sure you respect that.

The reason I like to share case histories is to give you real life examples. Everything that I will share with you I have learned firsthand.

Some insights and strategies I discovered through my experiences in life. Others come from the great teachings from my mentors, leaders of industry and specialists in their fields. Those who have taken me under their wing and others whom I've paid handsomely to glean gold nuggets. I will share wisdoms with you. Ideas, some beyond measure and some that are distinctly measurable that have improved my own financial and productive world.

The first thing you must do is stop using time and money as an excuse. These excuses limit your life and instead, use time and money well to reach your goals in life. As you courageously stop using time and money as excuses, this will be one new measure of success.

Success in life is not just HOW MUCH you put into your day; a great life comes from WHAT you put into your day.

Therefore, I ask you to commit to reading this book until the end, and just to be sure perhaps read it again. I've made it long enough to give value, but short enough so that you could read it in a day. I too have packed it with pertinent points for you to highlight, underline, so that you can use these to improve your time and money.

Sure, some of the concepts and strategies that I will share with you, will take you time to make those all-important shifts. Others you can apply immediately to make a huge difference to how much you get done in your day. My *5x5 To Thrive* for example will help to improve your productivity and focus enormously. It's near the end of the book, but please don't jump ahead and miss all the leading chapters. Because you will miss so much that will add to your *5x5 To Thrive* experience.

After-all, success in life is not just HOW MUCH you put into your day; a great life comes from WHAT you put into your day. Its quality over quantity. Aristotle said, "Excellence is a habit." There my friend is a clue to create the steppingstones to success. Put excellence, quality over quantity into your work and create a habit of it, and you are sure to succeed.

TIME SAVERS AND TIMELY QUESTIONS

1. The world conditions a weak mind. It will take advantage of your naïve soul if you let it. So, your life's mission is to strengthen your character and recondition your mind or face being conditioned to be someone's servant.
2. Stop using *time* and *money* as an excuse. These excuses limit your life and instead, use time and money well to reach your goals in life.

2. Your Diary Time Saver

Tony Robbins is a world authority on leadership. I attended his business mastery program in Sydney Australia to which he shared this story with me.

After he had written 'Awaken The Giant Within' he was offered the opportunity to join a small group of billionaires on their annual pilgrimage. Each year a group of influential billionaire businesspeople would charter a plane and fly off to an exotic location to spend time with one another. The aim was always to share ideas and opportunities to increase their wealth.

At the time, Tony wasn't the billionaire he is today. Nervously, he asked what it would cost. I can't imagine Tony being nervous at all today and don't remember the figure he shared with me. I think it was

somewhere in the vicinity of US$50,000. Though I do recall the response he got to his question, "Don't ask what it costs. An opportunity like this doesn't fall into just anyone's lap. Instead ask 'what could be gained from investing your time with billionaires?'"

The biggest excuses we place before our success often centres around money and time.

I'll say it again. The biggest excuses we place before our success often centres around money and time.

This book's intention is to give you a deep understanding of your greatest asset—time. But if you think this book is all about time, think again.

Using your time productively, effectively is the outcome. Though I'm far more interested in *what* determines the best outcomes. I hope you are too.

Conditioning your mind to be efficient is more than a psychological game. It's a transformational game —a game of turning your thinking around.

What will help you to get the most out of your day is what you put into your mind to create a discipline. Not just what you put into your day. Conditioning your mind to be efficient is more than a psychological game. It's a transformational game—a game of turning your thinking around.

To do that, you can't just read this book. It will be more helpful if you use it as guide to form new habits and that's the game of brain untraining. What you will need is to have your concept of time challenged. You will need new strategies and new reasons to get better results.

I continue to use these strategies to generate healthy profits from small teams. I first learned these in my role as a Creative Director of Advertising Agencies. I perfected them as the Training Director for *Life Beyond Limits*. Using these strategies allows me to generate huge profits from small teams. Productivity is the key to the longevity and profitability of my company *Life Beyond Limits*.

You too will increase your productivity and profitability using time. But not how most people view time. When you understand time in a new way, you will improve how you use it.

Though I'll say in advance. I'm going to be raw and real. No fluff or padding this journey out for you. It's about saving time after all.

**Show me an empty diary and
I'll show you an empty life.**

So let me start by saying. "Show me an empty diary and I'll show you an empty life." I know, it's quite a confrontational way to start a book, but there it is. I make no excuses for my 'in your face' writing style. Other than saying getting real is what we all need these days. No-one benefits from unproven theories. I'm about transforming lives and theories won't cut it. As real as I like to be, I am also kind.

So, there will be no grandstanding or daggers in the heart here.

Besides being a Director of *Life Beyond Limits Pty Ltd*. I am also a professional coach and coach trainer. Because I am, it is in my nature to care about you and humanity at large. Since 2002, I've been coaching people every week. I have trained groups for the corporate world and the public for the last 18 years. At the time of writing, I've dedicated over 38,000 hours of transformational work. That's an average of 1,900 hours every year. Some days I start early in the morning with my international clients and work until late in the evening. Time is important to me, and I must use it wisely.

I work with people who demand a change in their lives. When I'm not coaching or teaching, I'm writing books or researching. I've dedicated most of my life to work out how we tick and how we can improve. I'm busy and I'm guessing that because you're reading this, you are too.

The quality of your life comes down to what you schedule in your diary.

I can tell you right here and now that **the quality of your life comes down to what you schedule in your diary**. Your diary will play a key role in getting the most out of your day and your life.

Most people put work appointments in their diary. Others put social gatherings and these two groups will live completely different lives. Some put a balance of both social and professional tasks and appointments in their diary.

For me? I put *everything* in my diary. Everything that I want to get done. Social appointments, coaching sessions, training times, ideas for a new book. I'll even include a *YouTube* that I want to produce in the future, things that I want to start, continue or finish. I also block out important 'me time.' Everything that I want in my life goes into my diary! Everything!

What this does for me that works, is it helps me to be focused and productive. Super productive, purposeful, and profitable.

I don't know about you, but I have a purpose in this lifetime. I want to improve the lives of twenty million people in my lifetime. That's my life's goal.

What are your life goals? Do you have some? Do you have one? Do you have any? Goals are important, but more about that later.

Then the next question is this. If you have a big vision for your life, then, what is your strategy to achieve it? More-so, have you scheduled the strategic tasks as key entries into your diary? Planning your time is key to achieving anything in life and it keeps your mind orderly and avoids overwhelm.

Most people live haphazard destinies and so unstructured lives. I'm sure you know this. I see this in coaching all the time. People come to me to help them to get over their issues and reach their goals. Often the key is to bring some order into their lives, careers and businesses that are in chaos. Planning your time and using your diary is crucial.

I remember learning some insider tips on productivity from one of my early mentors. He said, "Touch it once." He loved people watching. One of his observations were that his employees would often use their time poorly. They would look at a task they had to do, then get to a complex part of the it and promptly find a distraction. Then return to the task later to give it another shot. Only to find themselves at the next challenge to seek another distraction. "The amount of time people waste would horrify them if they somehow had a time-waste recorder" he would say.

> **"Successful people make decisions quickly and change them slowly. While unsuccessful people make decisions slowly and change them quickly"** – Napoleon Hill

---

My mentor's strategy was to prioritise his tasks and stick to a task until it's done or at least a good section of it. He said, "This takes diligence and decisiveness." This came from his motto that he would share with me with regularity. To drill it into my head somehow. He said, "Successful people make decisions quickly and change them slowly. While unsuccessful people make decisions slowly and change them quickly" he would say.

Later I learned that his motto came from Napoleon Hill's *Keys to Success*.

I recall while working for *News Limited*. Each June I received my financial year diary. Each July I would invest hours of my time (or someone else's time), copying over all the key information from one diary to another. Birthdays, key meetings, important information and so forth would all be entered into my diary again, and again each year. Same data, different diary. It was a huge time waster. Today I use an electronic desktop diary that synchronises to my phone and all my computers. I make one appointment; one entry and it synchronises to all my systems.

Technology I recognise for some can be a curse, though I find it a blessing, mostly. I recall the days of what we would irritatingly call 'phone tag.' The game of calling each other, until finally we got to speak to one another. Often leaving messages on answering machines and services. Speaking to the same assistants again and again to schedule just one meeting or catchup.

These days, most people expect a text message even before making the phone call! Not to mention the multiple ways we leave messages these days. *Facebook Messenger*, texts, *What's App*, *Twitter* Messaging and you know that the list goes on and on.

One tool I love is *YouCanBookMe*. I give all my clients my diary links and they can access my diary and make a time to talk. Instead of continually missing each other by leaving phone calls.

For convenience, I have a link for my coaching clients to book a session. Once they have the link, they can access my diary and book a time. They can do this at any time, 24/7. We even created a link for people who want to talk to me about coaching. Even the link itself is clear what it's for: https://free-chat-with-rik.youcanbook.me/[1].

Successful people don't manage their time. They plan their time.

My entire life is planned and managed. I still get asked, "How do you get so much done?" To which I respond, "I don't manage my time, I plan my time." There's nothing to really manage as it's all planned out.

If time is important to you and you want to truly own your own life, then you've got the right book. So, let's invest some good time to save you time and get more from your time.

At the end of each chapter, I'm going to give you something to do to solidify the value of this book. I hope you don't mind a couple or a few tasks to improve your time. Let's start.

TIME SAVERS AND TIMELY QUESTIONS

1. Digitise your diary if you haven't already and synchronise it to all your devices. I use YouCanBookMe, though Calendly is good too.
2. Put all tasks that you want to start and finish in your diary too. Including strategic tasks that help you to reach your goals.
3. Touch it once. Practice picking up a task and finishing it to a stage of completion or complete it altogether.

# 3. Time: Your Only Limited Resource

Retired U.S. Army four-star General Stanley McChrystal organises his mornings with military precision.

Stan, as he put it, is "a pretty organised person." His entire day is usually booked up with work. So, he chooses to wake up at 4:00 am every day to get a ninety-minute workout in before he heads into the office. (He did an equally strenuous, and early morning workout routine when he was deployed in Iraq and Afghanistan.)

When I asked Stan how we can improve our own morning routines? Particularly with his military background in mind, he had this to say:

"Find certain things you know you should do, don't like to do, or make excuses to avoid, and then do them every day or every other day, and then it just becomes a habit."[1]

Some people achieve a great deal in a day, while others hardly achieve at all.

Others make millions in a day, while the majority of us make enough to get by. Though the one common ingredient we all have is time. We all have 24 hours in a day. We all have seven days in a week. No-one person gets any more or any less time. Though it's how you view time and how you use time that makes all the difference.

Differences? Differences to what you might ask. Well, consider this. Where you dedicate your time and focus is where you will gain your best results. Do you need to commit more time to your health? How are you going in the wealth stakes? Does your relationship need a little more focus? Time well spent can be time well invested.

Though the question that I would like to ask you is this. How do you see time? Is it something that you must give or is it something that gives to you?

If you feel that time is something that you must give, then you my friend, may well be a prisoner of time? Time is a burden, a penance, or a commitment that you have to give to others. You have lost your control of time. Your time is no longer yours.

Though conversely, do you believe that time gives to you? You may then consider the things you do with your time as adding value to your skills or your assets. You may consider time as an opportunity to progress that project or idea that you're building. This typically is the attitude of someone who is on purpose or has a purpose. How we perceive time is exactly how time shows up in our lives.

While those who believe time is something they must give, they may give over their time to other's passion or purpose. Consider this for moment.

Are you in a job you don't enjoy?

Have you volunteered your time to a board or a cause you no longer believe in?

Have you lost faith or trust of your associates?

Then my big question to you is this. What are you doing investing your time in things that no longer resonate with you? Why stay where you are no longer invested?

Yes, your emotional state says a lot about your time efficiencies but more about that later. So, let's look at time in another way.

How you view time determines how much you get from life.

Some people imagine time as days. Others see time in weeks. Yet, leaders with high productivity see time in minutes, and hold a vision for their output.

In other words, they assign small blocks of time to get tasks done, rather than long durations of time. They remain vigilantly focused on their overall mission.

While allocating small blocks of time to people tasks works for leaders and managers. It rarely works for project-oriented people. As they often need to focus on one project to get it done on time, to allow other teams to take up the next tasks.

Another way to look at time is through your purpose or your vision. Those who tend to get more from time have a vision that extends beyond their lifetime, and they value every minute. These can be some interesting ways to view time don't you think? Though we will talk about time a little later in more purposeful ways.

TIME SAVERS AND TIMELY QUESTIONS

1. Ask yourself, "Do I give my time or does time give to me?
2. If so, what I am using my time for? Do I have a grander purpose or even a soul purpose?
3. Am I doing too many things that are taking me away from my purpose?
4. Am I creating good habits with my time?

4. How Do You Measure Your Time?

Following Jack's adventures as a boy, years after climbing beanstalks and stealing golden egg laying geese from giants, Jack was asked a question. A life defining question from a young boy, a hero worshiper.

The young boy asked Jack, "How do you know how much time you have left?" To which Jack replied, "That's simple. You look at the length of your shadow." The boy hurriedly responded, "Then judging by your shadow that's getting longer by the second, either the sun is fading fast or that giant behind you is about to swiftly shorten your time!"

Excuse extending my creative liberty with one of the classics. But my point is this. How much time do you have left and how would you know?

Any day now could be your last; my last. Yet so many of us waste our days and so our lives, working in jobs we loathe, often for people we don't even like. How do I know this?

85% of people are unhappy in their jobs.

A global poll conducted by *Gallup* recently uncovered that out of the world's one billion full-time workers, only 15% of people are engaged at work. That means that an astronomical 85% of people are unhappy in their jobs.[1]

Conversely, while there are those who hate their jobs, there are those who cannot be stopped and won't go home! Though the difference between the productivity of these two groups is staggering. Though let's let some wind out of the balloon of passion and call those passionate players, happy. It stands to reason that if you're passionate about what you do, you are more likely to be happy in your work.

Economists at the *University of Warwick* found that happiness led to a 12% spike in productivity, while unhappy workers proved 10% less productive.

"Conventional wisdom holds that if only we pay workers enough, they'll be productive. There may be more to it, though. Recent research hints there's a link between employees' happiness and their productivity at work. Some companies are taking note—and already seeing the payoff.

"A recent study by economists at the *University of Warwick* found that happiness led to a 12% spike in productivity, while unhappy workers proved 10% less productive. As the research team put it, 'We find that human happiness has large and positive causal effects on productivity. Positive emotions appear to invigorate human beings.'"[2]

However, happy people and unhappy people can claim to be time poor.

Have you ever heard someone say, "I don't have the time?" How does one determine that they no longer have time? Shouldn't they be moving quicker? After-all, their life is about to run out!

Why do they look miserable and not stressed out of their heads? I would certainly be a little stressed if I discovered that I no longer have time.

The truth is that people talk in metaphors and play them out as if their metaphors were somehow true. When they are clearly not.

Metaphorically they're saying, "I am allocating my time to something more important than you or this conversation." It might sound a little rude, but it's true. We again, can only assume that because they're not laying there, dead on the floor.

The truth is that people talk in metaphors and play them out as if their metaphors were somehow true. When they are clearly not.

Sometimes we can listen to people's metaphors assuming that what they are sharing is real, when it's not.

Worse, because they are using the metaphors, they are likely to believe in their own stories.

For example, have you heard people say, "I'm trying to get over it." Like there is some monstrously high hurdle that is standing in front of them, obstructing their path. But there isn't.

Perhaps someone shared that, "Working through this project is like wading through tar." You might not be staring down at your feet right now, but it paints a bleak picture.

The problem with metaphors is that we come to believe them. Worse, the metaphors often suggest that we may as well quit right here and now or at least continue the drama.

Such as when someone says, "He's as thick as two planks of wood!" Will have us dismiss him as stupid, never allowing him to become anything else.

Sure, we can measure time and people in metaphors, but how else can you measure the duration of time?

We know that some archaeologists believed the complex patterns of lines on the desert floor in Nazca, Peru were used to mark celestial time. In North America we have found medicine wheels; stone circles dating from over 1,000 years ago. These may have been used to follow heavenly bodies as they moved across the sky over a year.

Variations and vagaries in the Earth's rotation eventually made astronomical measurements of time. Though these were inadequate for scientific and military needs that required highly accurate timekeeping. Today's standard of time is based on atomic clocks. Clocks that operate on the frequency of internal vibrations of atoms within molecules. These frequencies are independent of the Earth's rotation and are consistent from day to day within one part in 1,000 billion.

But that's how the ancients and science measure time, but how do you measure your time? How do you measure it and by what do you measure it?

You may work eight hours each day, every Monday to Friday, but how do you measure it in value and duration?

You may well sleep eight hours each night, but how do you measure it in value and duration?

You may work eight hours each day, every Monday to Friday, but how do you measure it in value and duration?

You may be about to do a talk, on stage to an audience of 10,000 people, now how do you measure your time in value and duration? Think of a performer who is being called to the stage at the Grammys for a three-minute acceptance speech?

If you aimed to put yourself in their shoes, chances are you were again measuring the value by your feelings. But you could also measure the time by the knock-on effect, the consequent value of that one talk or acceptance speech. When you try this on (so to speak), you come to realise that time is rarely measured by duration, although that's what most people think right off the cuff.

Some things you do have much greater value, albeit less duration of time.

Back in 2004, I was being mentored by a rising star in the training and self-development space. His name is Christopher Howard and Chris who he prefers to be known is American. Prior to meeting Chris, I learned Neuro Linguistic Programming or NLP. I knew a little about NLP but decided to complete my training with him.

When you measure time by value, not duration, you can change your financial fortune.

Chris had wisely invested his time. He knew that learning NLP was one thing but selling it was something entirely different. So, Chris focused intently to learn how to market and sell his offerings, which turned his life around. He went from robbing Peter to pay Paul (there's another metaphor). Before meeting Chris, he rented a house that was about to be demolished, to become a multi-millionaire.

He gave me his time, but I didn't pay him by the hour. I paid him for his value (I hope a light-globe went *POP!!* for you then).

Before meeting Chris, I worked tirelessly posting on social media to get clients. Did that work? Hell no.

Chris showed me how to get up on a stage for a few hours and make more money than I earned from months of working in my office. It's a paradigm shift. A strange concept if you've never done anything like it before. I never did! But here's the strange thing. I realised that I had been doing things my way for months and not getting anywhere. So, I said, 'Yes' and listened to every word of his golden advice. Even though most of it, at first, made no sense to me. Though it didn't stop me from taking massive action like a willing mentee.

I followed his guidance and guess what? I made millions! Not at first, but eventually his strategies worked for me too. Particularly as I perfected the art of his science. I made his strategies my own. Today, I teach coaches and trainers in our *Speaker Training*[3] and *Trainer Training*[4], how to do the same thing. I teach them the same thing that Chris taught me.

When you measure time by value, not duration, you can change your financial fortune. I did.

Small shifts in our thinking can sometimes create the biggest outcomes in our lives.

Small shifts in our thinking can sometimes create the biggest outcomes. That's why I put this short book together for you. I would like you to learn how to not only value your time but get more value from it. While most people think that you have to write a BIG book to make a BIG difference, I'm no longer one of them. I know that even a little book can make a BIG difference. I don't write for word count; I write for value. This is a concept that I would like you to understand—value.

What I'm sharing with you right now are philosophical shifts and we'll start layering these as ideas as we progress through this book.

When you focus your day on value, instead of time, the value of your day improves. That value can be to you or others, it doesn't matter. But let me take this much further for you and you will learn how to build a life of purpose, rather than a life of time.

As a Coach, to help my clients make more money and live a life of purpose, I usually start with this question, "Do you wish to have a career or a calling?" How you answer will make a big difference to the quality of your life.

> "You can't improve what you don't measure"
> – Peter Drucker

Finally, if you can't measure progress, then how do you know if you're really progressing? Described as 'the founder of modern management' Peter Drucker invented the concept known as 'management by objectives and self-control.' He had a saying which I think ends this chapter nicely, "You can't improve what you don't measure" – Peter Drucker.

So, my questions to you now are these…

TIME SAVERS AND TIMELY QUESTIONS

1. Ask yourself, "Are you measuring your time by value, not duration?"
2. What could you focus on instead in your day that are higher value tasks?
3. How can you measure your progress? Will you measure it by satisfaction? Income? Percentage of achievement in relation to your goals? What will be your most valuable measure?

5. A Career or Calling?

Back in 2007, I found myself in Bali at an entrepreneurs' business conference. There I met so many amazing people. The evenings that at times went into the wee hours of the morning in passionate conversation were as special as the conference itself. We found ourselves in all sorts of deep discussions.

I recall one evening where the topic of a 'calling' versus a 'career' came up. We all nodded in unison and agreed that Mother Teresa had a calling. Of course, Gandhi and Martin Luther King Jr. both had a calling. Then a usually quieter, elder gentleman in our group looked at me and said, "Your mother had a calling."

I must have had one of those quizzical looks because he leaned forward towards me and increased his volume.

"You're an author and change agent. You don't for one second think that your mother had nothing to do with that?"

His point rippled across the table. We all fell silent. His white hair shone a hallo in that moment as we all agreed. Gandhi's mother had a calling as much as Mother Teresa's mother and Martin Luther King Jr's. did. Of course, their fathers did too.

When it comes to our calling, many of us are not called to make news or run for the presidency. We are not called to start a non-profit or become a professional athlete. Our callings are perhaps geared toward something more personal and focused.

And yet, don't we tend to think of a calling differently? When you hear about a person having a calling, isn't it often someone doing grand, evident, and unusual things?

We can come to believe that a calling is only for special, world-class people. We sense a separation between the great lives we read about, and the ordinary things that make up our lives. Having and following a calling can seem like something for other people, but not for us. Though I promise you, we all have the opportunity to be called. The question is, do we listen and respond?

Some people think ahead. Some people think in the past. Some people live in the present. I'm none of those.

I know that people who live in the past are usually filled with regret or at least, wishing to relive the past. While those who live in the future risk anxiety. While some arrive at their outcome disappointed at not meeting their expectations. That used to be me, but I've coached that idea right out of me.

Then there are those who always think ahead. They live in the future and are usually filled with angst, trying to get everything they do in the now to be perfect. Absolutely

EVERYTHING! I promise you, everything you do doesn't count. Some things you do add value while so many don't.

Me? I prefer to think in the moment; in the present and plan for a thousand years. Okay, I hear you. I know what you're saying, "A thousand years! Are you for real?" I'm very real. Check out my photo and bio at the back! (That's a joke by the way. I really don't need you to do that).

But seriously, let me show you how this works. Oh! And by the way, it's not my idea. I got this from another of my mentors and I got it from one of those great value questions you get asked by great mentors. Here's the question.

"If you think in one-thousand years, how many people were born in order for you to be here?"

Actually, let *me* be your mentor and ask it of you. There are three questions. Here's the first one. "If you think in one-thousand years, how many people were born in order for you to be here?"

Now I know that's a doosey of a question, isn't it? Sorry, that was another question, wasn't it? Okay, I'll stop it now, but seriously, "If you think in one-thousand years, how many people were born in order for you to be here?"

Let me stop you before you break-out your abacus or pull out all the contents of your closet to find that scientific calculator of yours. The answer is A lot!

A great many people were born in the last thousand years so that you could be born. Grandparents, great grandparents, great-great grandparents and so-forth and soon. You get it. There were so many people who had to be born in your lineage, for you to be here reading this book.

So, here's my second question...

"Of all the people who were born over the last thousand years for you to be right here... What *legacy* did any of them leave?" Any monuments? Any major assets? An heirloom perhaps? A Monet? A Tom Roberts landscape? A paint-by-numbers by granny? A book? Family fortunes? A family business? Any legacies? Any at all? None? Nothing? Nada?

Do you know what the answer is?

The answer is, YOU! You are the answer to the second question. You are the legacy that came from all those people in your family line. You are the one that was born, perhaps to honour your entire family? Well, that's how I feel anyway.

Okay then. You're ready for the third and final question.

I will say in advance that this is the most important question of all. Not to put any pressure on you or anything. But it's important. So here it is.

"What legacy will you leave?"

BOOM! There's the power of that question right there!

I hope these three questions have got you thinking? I hope this book so far has got you thinking. That's a big part of my purpose—to get you thinking in new ways.

When asked, "What do you do?"
Most people espouse their job titles or recite their CV.

While most people, when asked what I do, usually respond with things like...

"He's a Coach and a Brain Untrainer. He helps people to change problematic ways in which people think. He's helped people with anxiety and depression completely disappear. He's made some people rich, wise, happy. Oh! He's written some books and he's a Master trainer of NLP, Life Coaching, Speakers and Trainers." Then they may even add, "He's an accredited trainer with the Neuro Linguistic Programming Association of Australia Incorporated (NLPAA)."

Then some might say, "He's a radio announcer with Sapphire FM. He's got a show called, 'What's On Your Mind.'" These are not the things I do; these are HOW I do what I do, not WHO I am.

It's typically the first thing that most people say when asked, "What do you do?" Most people espouse their job titles or recite their CV.

Imagine, that when asked, "What do you do?" You instead quote the legacy you are aiming to leave behind?

**We are and will all be judged
upon how we met other peoples' values.**

Now in truth. While all the descriptions of what I do are all true, they're subjective. They're generic titles and projects. They're not considering or even matching the values that the observer may hold dear. In other words. We are and will all be judged upon how we met other peoples' values. Oh! There's that 'value' word again. People really don't care about our job titles and the projects we're working on. They care about the bigger picture—the WHY we do what we do.

Why do you do what you do? Is there a bigger purpose or a bigger reason?

If you want bigger results, find a bigger reason.

If you find yourself straddling the hamster wheel of life (another metaphor!)? This then may be just a signal to you, that you haven't found your purpose or reason.

When you find your reason, you will find it much easier to get bigger or better results from your time. This caused me to arrive at a saying, "If you want bigger results, find a bigger reason."

You will know the difference if you have a calling, instead of a career. If you have a calling, your time will feel more purposeful and have more meaning. You will likely invest more time in a calling than a career. Chances are you will awaken earlier and go to bed later. It is likely you will never tire. You may even choose to never retire. Why would you? It's more of a WHY question than a WHAT question. It's not about WHAT you do but WHY you do it.

Some people make a living, while others make a life worth living.

Some people make a living, while others make a life worth living.

I am everything people say I am. Who am I to argue? It's only their opinions and values after all. But who I really am is someone who cares deeply about the future of humanity. I care about what our leaders will do in the next thousand years. I want to do everything I can to create a kinder world. I will do everything in my power to influence humanity. You may have noticed that I like to sprinkle my books with kindness and humanness. I intentionally add a moral code, a thought for humanity. I too hope that someone is reading this book, gleaning some insights and kindness long after I'm gone.

That's why I will continue to write books, do videos to educate. To change how people think. I will coach, teach, and speak. All of this is *how* I do what I do. What I do to inspire humanity to be their better selves. To truly care about the planet and its future. I personally think that it starts with an awakening. Just like I hope you're having an awakening now. But then ultimately, we must move from being awakened, to taking kinder actions. The kind of action that inspires others to follow your lead. Thoughtful actions that bring about harmony among us all.

Steve Jobs stood in front of the 2005 Stanford graduating class and said, "The only way to do great work is to love what you do," but how does enjoying your work really lead to success in the workplace?

Being happy at work and loving what you do is an overall productivity booster and enhances performance. People who enjoy their jobs are more likely to be optimistic, motivated, learn faster, make fewer mistakes, and better business decisions.

The old school of management was all about starting fire under people.

The new school of leadership is all about starting fire inside people.

"In a recent research, Yuna Cho of the University of Hong Kong and Winnie Jiang found evidence that calling-oriented employees nevertheless do actually tend to achieve higher pay and organisational status. So, if they're not necessarily doing a better job, why are these professionals more successful? Their research indicated that it's because managers tend to be biased toward those with a calling orientation.

"In the first, we tapped into the Wisconsin Longitudinal Study (WLS), a long-term data collection effort that measures life outcomes in a random sample of Wisconsin high school graduates from 1957.

"Participants of the study were surveyed on their work orientation in 2004. Among the 1,077 respondents to this survey, 49% identified as having a calling orientation, 35% identified as having a job orientation, and 16% said they worked primarily for career advancement.

"After controlling for demographic, socioeconomic and employment-related characteristics, they found that those who had found their calling at work tended to earn more than those who worked for compensation or status.

"Researchers found that participants were more likely to assign a higher bonus and raise to calling-oriented people ($675; 4.36%) than job-oriented people ($630; 3.95%). These differences are statistically significant. Calling-oriented people was also most likely to be recommended for promotion."[1]

According to Mihaly Csikszentmihalyi, a distinguished Hungarian psychologist, being able to enjoy your work is the main factor in getting into a state of flow.

Flow is the experience you have when you are 'in the zone.' You feel fully focused, creative, and ideas are flowing freely.

This means that every time you are given a task and view it negatively, this mindset is already making it harder for you to complete your work. Doing work you love is energizing and creates a positive feedback loop that fuels productivity. Your passion for the work energises you and vice versa, giving you more fuel to put towards success. The trick is figuring out how to make yourself love your work—even the most tedious of tasks.

Csikszentmihalyi discovered that once you take on a task with a positive mindset and think of the benefits you can reap from completing this project, your work is more likely to happen in a steady, concentrated flow. Being in this state of mind means you will be highly focused and fully absorbed in the task at hand, just as you would be while doing something you really enjoy. Being able to fully devote yourself to a task and give it your all will make you more productive and knowledgeable, leading you towards success at work.

So, in summary, if you feel more purposeful in your time, such as thinking of the benefits one thousand years from now, your time will become more valuable.

Can you think well beyond your lifetime and act in the present? I hope so because we will all benefit. Of course, planning your time will be an enormous help. So, let me continue to help you to do that.

TIME SAVERS AND TIMELY QUESTIONS

1. Answer these three questions: Here's the first one. "If you think in one-thousand years, how many people were born in order for you to be here?"
2. Here's your second question: "Of all the people who were born over the last thousand years for you to be right here... What *legacy* did any of them leave?" And finally, your third question:
3. "What legacy will you leave?

6. More Value Equals More Time

A philosophy professor decided to teach his students a valuable lesson about Time Management. He stood before his class with some items on the table.

When the class began, without speaking, he picked up a big empty jar. Then he proceeded to fill it to the top with rocks about the size of small plumbs. He then looked towards the class and asked the students if the jar was full. They all agreed it was full.

With a slight smirk, the professor moved back to pick up a box of pebbles and poured them into the jar. He shook the

jar gently. The pebbles rolled through the gaps between the rocks.

He then again looked up to the students and holding up the jar for all to see, asked if the jar was full. Again, they all nodded their heads in agreement.

For the last time, he turned towards a box and picked up a box of sand and poured it into the jar and shook it lightly. Of course, the sand moved into the gaps and filled up everything else.

He then asked one last time if the jar was full or not. The students were surprised but responded with a unanimous "Yes."

"Now," said the professor, "I want you to consider that this jar is a metaphor for your life. The rocks are the important things. Your family, your children, your health, your partner. Things that are your everything, your most highly valued people in your life. If nothing remained but only these then your life would still be full.

The pebbles are the other things that matter—like your job, your career, your house.

The sand is everything else. The small stuff. The unimportant stuff."

"If you put the sand (unimportant stuff) into the jar first," he continued "there is no space for the pebbles (career, job) or the rocks (family, children). Choose what is important and place your value appropriately and with priority."

To claim more time in your day might sound like a challenge but really, it's not all that hard. It's just a decision. But what do I need to decide you might ask?

That's a very good question. So, here's my answer. You need to decide that your time is valuable. While you might be thinking right now; "What do I do that is of any value to anyone?"

Start thinking like you are in someone else's shoes. Heels? Thongs? You get the idea.

Think to yourself, "When I do that thing that I do; whatever it is you do; who values it most?" Who gets the biggest bang for my time? Are you still thinking, "What value?" Okay. Let me give you an example or two to help.

My wife Rebecca loves cooking. She values her skill and talent in the kitchen. Why? Well first let me say that this example that I am about to use does not marginalise my wife in any way. On the contrary. So please don't go all 'this is sexist' on me because you'll miss my point.

Truth be known, everyone in my family cooks, including me. So back to my point.

Can you remember that complimentary line in that old Australian classic movie, 'The Castle?' You know the one? When Daryl Kerrigan, the family's father says about his wife Sal Kerrigan's cooking, "Wow! That looks lovely darl. What do you call that?" Of course, Sal responds with an 'Aw shucks,' coy and simple, "Sponge cake."

While you might be thinking that's a bit trite or lame. Let me continue.

The talents that will grow are the ones that are appreciated.

Each night, Sal Kerrigan continues to deliver value to a grateful and thankful Kerrigan family. Why? Because Sal's skill and actions is valued by her family.

You could only imagine that each time she cooks, she smiles inside, knowing in anticipation, the gratitude she is about to receive.

My wife is a great cook because simply she is. But we tell her she is. Often! Now that's not her only talent. She's a great gardener, an insightful coach, a brilliant energy healer and wonderful mother to our daughters, and she's a thoughtful and caring wife to me. Just to name a few of her positive traits and talents. But here's my point. The talents that we grow are so often the very same talents that are appreciated.

When you value what you do with your time or the outcome of your time spent, your time increases in value. Think about it this way. The time that it takes Sal Kerrigan to cook a meal may be 30 minutes or an hour or more. The time that it takes the Kerrigan's to have their evening meal might be 30 minutes, at most. But the good feelings that come from let's call it an hour of that day and the gratitude of her family could last in her heart forever.

Let's look at this conversely.

Now imagine the Rotten family. Mr. and Mrs. Rotten have been slaving in the kitchen for hours preparing the family's Christmas dinner. Finally, the family arrive at the table to scoff down their meal and afterwards complain profusely about it.

"The turkey's as dry as a dog's bone! My steak's as tough as an old boot! These asparagus look like limp d#@ks!" Sorry for swearing. I really want to make a point here. Think of all the time that Mr. and Mrs. Rotten spent preparing dinner and the results they achieved. Pretty soon, if not now, Mr. and Mrs. Rotten will become resentful. While future dinners may be sparse or quickly put together. That short time that it takes to cook will endure as a life filled with resentment.

Now put yourself in Sal Kerrigan's shoes. How does that time feel? Then compare that by putting yourself in Mr.

and Mrs. Rotten's old boots. What does your time feel like now?

Am I saying that time is a measure of a moment or a measure of a feeling? Think about that question. Truly ponder it. The value of time is so often measured by our feelings.

When you remember your time, what determines if it was well-spent or wasted? That's right! It's the value of it and how you *feel* about it as a result.

How you feel is more important than what you earn.

I recall talking to my trainer Chris about where I was thinking of niching my coaching and I had designed an amazing process to help people quit smoking. I say 'amazing' as I since have used this process on hundreds of clients, and it works 80% of the time.

Chris asked me what I wanted to charge to deliver the process and I said, "I think $350 for the three-hour session seemed fair." He laughed and said, "No-one is going to take you seriously at $350. I'd be charging $5,000." To which I almost spluttered my response. Remember, back then I had some serious money issues. I didn't know the true value of money or genius. But I get it now. These days, the average smoker pays AUD$3,212 per year on cigarettes[1]. That's just what costs for the cigarettes and not the health or social costs. Today I get where Chris is coming from, and these days I charge AUD$4,400 for the process.

Consider what you do that delivers the greatest value to someone and you might just have a business or side hustle worth the time to pursue?

Time is not linear. It is filled with feelings, memories, value and also recognition of time spent. Let me explain.

New research on employee engagement examines the relationships among motivation, money, and recognition. It found that how you feel is more important than what you earn.

A key finding was that 70% of survey respondents reported their most meaningful recognition "had no dollar value." A substantial increase from 57% in a similar survey in 2007.

The study was funded by *Make Their Day*, an employee motivation firm, and *Badgeville*, a gamification company. They surveyed 1,200 U.S. employees from a broad cross-section of industries.

Among the study's highlights:

- 83% of respondents agreed, recognition for contributions was more fulfilling than any rewards or gifts.
- 76% found peer praise very or extremely motivating.
- 88% found praise from managers very or extremely motivating.
- 90% said a "fun work environment" was very or extremely motivating.

"Workers of all ages, especially the rising Millennial population," concluded Ken Comee, *Badgeville* CEO, "are motivated by real-time feedback, fun, engaging work environments, and status-based recognition over tangible rewards."[2]

This study supports what I have personally found to be true. Value comes down to how you *feel*. The better you feel, the more value you place on the time that is the cause of that feeling. You might have to read that again?

In September 2006 my father, Joseph Schnabel passed away at age 90. He was raised an orphan by nuns. He lived a life of war-torn tragedy as a prisoner of war. He was funny, witty and wise as those years could not take his spirit away. The essence of my father is one I will always keep close to my heart. He was kind man. While he worked tirelessly, and I never saw him that much growing up but the moments that I did, I still treasure. Those values were our philosophical chats. His key pieces of advice.

Though the moment I remember with most fondness was the day as a young child of three or four, he met me in the bathroom and saw my struggle to wash my hands. No-one ever taught me how to do that, until Dad. Dad grabbed my little hands in his, soaped up my hands and showed me how to wash my hands, meshing my fingers to make sure every skerrick of dirt was washed away and my hands were polished clean. That one moment held so much value to me. It showed me how much my dad cared. That one moment didn't last long, but because of its value, I will never forget it.

TIME SAVERS AND TIMELY QUESTIONS

1. Ask yourself, "What am I doing that isn't valued?" Perhaps your doing those tasks only to gain appreciation, that you never get?
2. Perhaps, stop doing them and save more time.
3. Consider what you do that delivers the greatest value to someone and you might just have a business or side hustle worth the time to pursue?

7. What's Your Power Time?

Let's power up your time. How can you do that? With what I call 'key drivers.' Key drivers are the things that make the biggest difference to your career, your business or your life. They can also be the most valuable things to do or to master.

In short, key drivers give you the biggest bang for your buck—or your time in this case.

This reminds me of a story that Siimon Reynolds, a colleague in advertising shared with me one day. The story centres around a blind beggar in a park.

One day, Siimon and a friend were walking together

through a park when they came upon a blind man. The man was sitting up with his back against a tree. In front of him was an upended hat with some scant coins within it. The blind man had positioned in front of his hat a sign that said, 'I'm blind.'

Siimon bent down so the blind man could hear him and said, "Good morning. My name is Siimon and I'm in advertising. Would you mind if I made a small addition to your sign which I think will make a huge difference to the donations you receive?" To which the blind man heard Siimon's trusting voice and responded, "Yes please."

After altering the blind man's sign, Siimon and his friend said goodbye only to see him again, up against the very same tree the following day. Though they noticed that the man had significantly more money in his hat. To which Siimon said, "Good morning." The blind man immediately recognised Siimon's voice and excitedly asked, "What did you add to my sign?"

Siimon said, "Your sign said 'I'm blind' and that was all. Knowing that yesterday was the first day of Spring, I added, 'It's Spring and...' your sign followed, 'I'm blind.'"

The story demonstrates that small, considered tasks can reap large rewards.

A key driver in getting results from your signs, your advertising, your email copy is relatability. So, if you wanted to get better results from your words a key driver might be to learn copywriting. If copywriting is going to make a huge difference, then it's worth the time.

We've spoken a great deal about time. We've also concluded that what you put into time has differing values. What is valuable to one person in time, may not be valuable to another. But let us now discuss 'Power Time.'

When I'm coaching my business clients to help them to increase their income, I have a key. I call this key, 'Key Drivers' and that's what I search for in our sessions. Key drivers are the activities that deliver the greatest returns for the least amount of energy, time or effort. One client that immediately springs to mind is Life Coach that had no idea how to get clients. Most coaches have no idea.

She didn't have a database, nor a social media following, let alone a large network. But she did have a small network. We scratched around looking for her key drivers to get clients and we discovered that one business owner in her network, a gentleman with a consulting business had a large database. We put a proposal to him to swap her coaching in return for him to send out one email blast for every coaching session she gave him. That one key driver, which she still uses, helped her to get her first 22 clients.

My own personal example of this is public speaking. Every time I stand up in front of an audience, I stand to make the most money. You learned this in one of the earlier chapters. Remember I spoke of my mentor Chris Howard, whom I learned this strategy from? Public speaking gets me a bigger financial return than any other strategy.

My key drivers include public speaking, interviews on podcasts and in the media. The more opportunities I get to do those activities in a year, the greater my income. Does that make sense to you?

You know as well as I do, that it is easy just to doddle through your days. In doing so, you soon discover that the squeakiest hinges get all the oil. The most vocal problems get the most attention. In fact, I have found that the more talented you are, the more you are asked to help. Now while feeling needed or valued can be great boost to your ego. You quickly discover that your ego is one of the most expensive elements you own. If you've completed our "Money Magic"[1] program, you'll know that our egos cost us a fortune!

I have another saying that I think may be helpful here. It's what I learned as a parent. While being there for your children is being responsible as a parent, it can debilitate your children too.

Whatever you do for your children is what they may not be able to do for themselves.

As you probably know, I coach people and families for all sorts of reasons. In my 20 years as a coach, I've helped my fair share of parents with problematic family situations. These are often caused by well-meaning parents. Parents who have indulged themselves in helicopter parenting or it's opposite.

While we think it's good to feel needed by our children and run to their side to help them at every opportunity. This can develop into a crippling co-dependence with our children. Yes, you know I like my sayings, but here it goes. "Whatever you do for your children is what they don't need to do for themselves."

Let us move on from oiling squeaking hinges and helicopter parenting and back to key drivers.

Your key drivers are activities that get you the best returns from your time invested. Now for me. While it might take me a lot more to time to prepare for an event or to speak on stage, than it does to send out an email blast. I know that public speaking delivers a greater financial reward. Let me share a quick story for you to clarify this one point.

Before the COVID-19 pan-panic happened. I got a phone call from the *National Speakers Association*. They asked me when I would next be in Melbourne. I looked at my diary and found the dates. Those dates corresponded to an opportunity to speak at one of their events. So, I said "Yes."

As the weeks got closer to my talk, I asked the office to arrange my accommodation. It was then that I discovered that our office got my Melbourne dates wrong.

Personally, I don't like to say one thing and do another. So, I made good on my promise and continued my arrangements to fly to Melbourne for the talk. Only to have to do it all over again the following week. Dang! I was going to have to pay to travel to Melbourne, meals, accommodation. All this to speak at an event for free. What the heck! I did it anyway.

I invested my time to craft a great talk for the audience which I entitled, "Words Of Wealth—the WHAT economy versus the HOW economy?"

You get power time when you discover your key drivers.

The talk was well-received. I saw light globes going off all over that room. In my head I thought, "Worst case scenario, my talk is landing with the room." Though it was a much smaller audience than I was used to, with a mere 20 or so people in attendance. I never sold a product (other than me). I never put together a package or offer. Though the net total of the revenue that came from that talk was upwards of 50 times what it cost me to be there and speak. People later contacted me and asked for my help. Even though I never offered anything that anyone could buy at that talk.

I have discovered, as a speaker, it is often financially better for me to speak without being paid. As long as I can sell from the stage. A speaker fee, without being able to sell is usually a poorer option. Let this land for you.

Public speaking is often a key driver for many businesses as it creates a distinct point of difference in your business. Books are also a great key driver for many.

Could you do something like this in your career or business to increase your revenue or escalate your credibility with 'Power Time?' You get power time when you discover your key drivers.

Key drivers are often the things that you do that leverage your value. In other words, my value is helping people to change how they think. Getting up in front of an audience is how I leverage that value.

The formula to wealth is VALUE x LEVERAGE.

At the risk of missing this point, I'll add the formula to wealth. It's simple. The formula is VALUE x LEVERAGE. Increase your value and then leverage your value to the largest audience or market possible. You can even leverage to a small niche audience and the formula will still work.

I would like to give you another example of key drivers so that you really get this chapter. Let's use someone like a mechanic. A mechanic for example may know how to fix car problems with lightning speed but can only fix one car at a time. To leverage that value, that mechanic could choose to create a course. A course that teaches other mechanics how to identify car issues faster. The value is the knowledge, and the leverage is the large number of mechanics that wish to learn.

Another way of looking at it, the mechanic could also take on more mechanics and earn a portion of their income. Though this means that they will likely need another key driver to their skills. The skill of marketing, managing people and the knowledge to run a larger business for example.

Back in the 80s, when I ran advertising agencies I learned about leverage. It took me almost a year, but the idea finally dawned on me. Once it did, I dramatically increased my income. To keep the math simple, it looked something like this.

Let's say I was earning $300 per hour. My value was producing advertising campaigns and designs for my clients. But there was just one of me and my partner Alan Knights who looked after sales. There was no such thing as leverage in this formula. We both only made money by exchanging our time. If anything, Alan's sales had more leverage.

Once I couldn't handle any more work, I searched for another person who had as much talent or more than I did. In other words, I employed more 'value.'

My first employee was paid $30 an hour (it was way back in the 80s after all). I billed him out to my clients for $300 an hour, but at first, I had to oversee his work. I earned $300 per hour, plus my new employee earned for us another $300 an hour, less the $30 we paid him. So, my hourly income rose to $570 an hour. My $300 and his $270 per hour.

Once my first staff member was at full capacity, I hired another team member and did the same thing. In a couple of months, I was now earning for each hour, my original $300 and two amounts of $270. Now instead of earning $570 and hour, I was earning $840 an hour.

Now let's assume that we billed every hour that year (which of course we didn't, but just for the simplicity of the math, stay with me). So that's $300 per hour, just for me. Let's multiply that over an 8-hour day x 5 days a week (40 hours). Then let us multiply that by 48 weeks (accounting for 4 weeks of holidays). This now equals 1,920 hours x $300 is now the figure at full capacity. That amount now comes to $576,000 annual gross. Now let's see what happens when we add my two extra employees?

So, let's add $300 per hour, less $30 comes to $270 x2 employees, which comes to $540. Now let's multiply that over 8-hour days x 5 days a week (40 hours) x 48 weeks (accounting for 4 weeks of holidays) equals 1,920 hours x $540. That new gross figure comes to $1,036,800, plus my income of $576,000. The total now comes to $1,612,800 gross. Now do you understand the power of value x leverage?

Of course, I had to expand my value to include the skills to run a bigger business and manage more staff.

Eventually we needed more team members. These included non-income producing staff such as a receptionist and a production manager. But once you get this concept, the next thing you'll need is the courage to think bigger. But before you go there. Let me ask you another question.

It makes sense to ask you now, what are your key drivers?

What activities deliver you the most income in the shortest time? Or the most joy in the shortest amount of time, if you are chasing a different outcome. What activities deliver you the most joy in the easiest way?

What thing do you need to focus on each day to improve your health in wonderful life extending ways?

The answer of course to these questions will lead you to your 'key drivers.' Though you now need to find out what are those key drivers?

The easiest way to start searching for your key drivers is to determine what is the outcome that you wish to achieve? Then consider, what will make that outcome shorter? Better? Faster? More profitable? Smarter? Easier? Then you are at the halfway point.

The next step is to use your knowledge or speak to someone who has achieved what you aim to do. Perhaps, get a mentor or a coach? You could also start tapping into your creative genius as the key drivers are often found there?

I'd like to finish this chapter with a key driver that I shared in my book, *A Richer Way to Think*[2]—and you'll soon see why I called it that. Here goes.

"A school had a problem with a group of 12-year-old girls who were starting to use lipstick. For fun they repeatedly kissed the toilet mirror above the hand basins. They left their lipstick marks all over the mirror.

The janitor was furious! He found the lipstick difficult to remove and was frustrated.

Each day he would clean the mirror, only to see them reappear the following day. Every day he felt his frustration and anger building as he approached the toilet.

The school tried countless ways to stop the girls until the headmaster intervened. Believing success was inevitable, the headmaster thought in richer ways. He came up with a solution.

The headmaster called all the girls into the toilet. He explained how difficult it was to clean off the lipstick. He then asked the janitor to demonstrate the level of difficulty. How did he do that? He dipped his mop into a nearby toilet and put it to the mirror, smudging the lipstick across the glass. The girls never kissed the mirror again."[2]

That my friend is leverage. Sometimes you keep trying the same thing without result, again and again. Leverage is like a fulcrum, where you don't need much effort to tip the scales in your favour. You sometimes just need to think creatively. Perhaps in richer ways.

TIME SAVERS AND TIMELY QUESTIONS

1. What activities deliver you the most income in the shortest time?
2. What activities deliver you the most joy in the easiest way?
3. What thing do you need to focus on each day to improve your health in wonderful life extending ways?
4. The easiest way to start searching for your key drivers is to determine what is the outcome that you wish to achieve? Then consider, what will make that outcome shorter? Better? Faster? More profitable? Smarter? Easier?
5. The next step is to use your knowledge or speak to someone who has achieved what you aim to do. Perhaps, get a mentor or a coach? You could also start tapping into your creative genius as the key drivers are often found there?

8. Your Time First

A wealthy man had invested most of his time learning how to make more money and getting busy on applying all he learned. While he was reasonably wealthy he had not achieved his dream of being absolutely financially free.

Getting rich took all his time. The man hardly had the time for his family. He thought to himself, that one day he would be rich and then give all his time to his family.

Though one evening, laying in his bed a rapid sickness took hold. Within minutes, he found himself above his body, pleading with the Angel of Death. Bargaining he said, "I'm not ready to die. If you can give me one more year to spend time with my family and friends, I promise to give one million dollars to charity." The Angel refused.

The dying man then asked, "If I give you half my wealth, can I have just one day with family?" Again, the Angel refused.

Finally, the dying man pleaded, "I will give you all my wealth for just one hour to play with my son. I haven't played with him in months." Finally, the Angel accepted, with a condition. The condition was that the dying man was to leave a note for his son, for what he learned in his life.

The man happily agreed. Wasting no time, he woke his son from his slumber and the child excitedly leapt out of bed and hugged his father. He then spent his final hour of life, happily playing with his son.

In the final remaining minutes of his life, he began writing a note which said, "Spend your time wisely. Because you never know what the next moment in time holds for you. Do the things you love. Spend time with your friends and your family. Spend time to admire the beauty of nature. No amount of money can buy you more time. So never postpone your happiness. Enjoy the moment and always follow your heart. Cherish every moment of your existence. Thank you. I will always love you. Dad xo."

While in the space of preservation and self-care it all makes sense. Though, how seldom do we apply that same motto to our lives on the ground?

Are you the kind of person who gives more than you receive? Do you find you're the go-to person when it comes to advice and help? When there's a problem, do you start scanning your brain immediately for a solution? Do you feel people's pain and try your best to relieve it? If you answered 'Yes' to any of these questions, chances are you are a giver. A giver cares more about others than they do about themselves and willingly offers their help.

As most of my work is with coaches, trainers, authors and speakers, my world is encircled by givers. These people are those who live to serve. They selflessly put other people before themselves. So, self-care among my tribe is uncommon and so, burnout is rife.

In the best interests of my clients and students, I will often raise the self-care issue and offer solutions. Yes, I'm a giver too so I have to make a conscious effort to give back to me. I have to consciously stop myself from giving. After all, here I am at 2:11 am in the morning typing these words for you. Here is one of my self-care strategies that works for my clients, and it's worked for me too for the last 14 years.

Earlier I spoke about the importance of my diary. Here is one strategy that I have found adds the all-important self-care regime into my weekly schedule. But before I go there, let me share why I developed this strategy.

Back in 2008 I was on a Virgin flight from Sydney, heading towards Melbourne. It was late and I had woken up to see the flight attendant smiling in front of me. She said, "You look so tired" to which I responded with a bedraggled, "Yes, I guess I am." She laughed and said, "You might want to thank the lady on your left and the gentleman on your right for them kindly donating their shoulders as pillows." They all erupted in laughter. I was still waking up.

As the laughter subsided, I said an embarrassed thanks to the lady and the gentleman on either side of me, and the cheery flight attendant. Though the real story was in the years leading up to that moment.

Sometimes we get so swept up in the ra ra of our goals and achievement that we forget ourselves.

You know I'm a Master Trainer of Neuro Linguistic Programming. You also know I teach Life Coaching and have now practiced as a commercial coach for 20 years. But back then, in 2008 on that flight to Melbourne, I had been coaching for only six years and teaching NLP for two years. I was a man on a mission.

I had created my goals. Written them down. I even created a couple of vision boards on artist canvases. My goals were also in picture form, hanging in my office. They were even blue-tacked next to my bathroom mirror on the wall as a constant reminder. They were everywhere! Best of all or so I thought, I was achieving them all so fast. So much so, that I had designed my ideal life and I was now living it or at least I thought so.

I achieved every one of my dreams but in the quiet humming of that plane, I asked myself, "Is this really the life I wanted? Did I truly want to be this busy?" Sometimes we get so swept up in the ra ra of our goals and achievement that we forget ourselves.

I mean, here I was, completely exhausted at the end of another busy day.

Monday to Friday, I typically got up at 6 am to coach my business clients starting at 7 am. From 9 am until 10 pm most days I then coached all kinds of people with all types of goals and issues. But today, I had to end my coaching at 5 pm to jump on a *Virgin* flight to Sydney so I could give a talk. Then back home to get some dinner and sleep.

Most weekends I ran workshops. Some weeks I taught our 8-day *Life Coach + NLP Practitioner* training or our 9-day *Master Coach + Master NLP Practitioner* training or *Speakers* or *Trainers* training. I was busy.

In-between all of that, I was still writing books and creating videos—and managing our team. Every now and again, I was able to take my family to Hawaii for a couple of weeks. Hawaii is our favourite holiday destination. Mind you,

I sometimes would do a talk while we were there and sometimes do an interview on a radio station or meet with a group. Though all holidays end and soon enough my crazy schedule continued. My days were nuts.

That weekend, after my Sydney flight, I had a weekend off and enjoyed the time with my family. Zoe, my daughter, was six years old at the time, and Sienna was about to turn three. Rebecca and I bundled up our kids to go out to one of our favourite breakfast haunts. Either St Kilda's *The Sandbar* on Beaconsfield Parade or Port Melbourne's *Café Zest*. We loved their Green Eggs and Ham.

At the time, we lived in Southbank in Victoria, Australia. I bought a large top floor apartment with a fireplace, which was quite unique. Rebecca and I loved to sit outside on our balcony that faced Southbank Boulevard. We would watch the world go by and often talk about our future or what's next. While I loved our life, I shared with Rebecca that I needed some me time. We needed more of us time too. Sure, we had our date nights, our Hawaiian Holidays and weekend getaways. But in all the work, I lost me in *Life Beyond Limits* and Rebecca lost herself to mothering. So, we started sharing some ideas.

I distinctly recall that it was Rebecca's idea that generated the biggest gasp. You know those moments when you suck a big gush of air in just before you share an aha? Rebecca said, "You know how we love those tropical places and all that outdoor living? And you know how you say that you don't think you will ever retire?" At this point I'm feeling the energy of it all and thinking, what's she up to? "Well," she continued, "Why don't we live the retirement life now?" To which my facial expression clearly said I didn't get it at all. Rebecca said, "Hear me out."

Rebecca went straight to it. "Why don't we move our entire business to Maui or Oahu?" My favourite place in the world is Maui, so I was immediately on board. My heart brain is saying, "Yes, yes, yes, yes, yes. That's a definite yes for me!" But my head brain is going, "Whaaaat? How's that going to work?"

Later in my career I was to learn how important it is to consider your heart brain, gut brain and head brain in making decisions. We even created an online course called the "3 Brain Integration."

So, are you saying that every person who lives in a city has blackened lungs from the road debris, dust and pollutants?

The final straw for us, living in the city happened after having a conversation with friends. Warren is a police officer, and his wife Cheryl is an ex-nurse. Warren shared that during his police training he visited the morgue.

Most of the time, police will investigate a deceased body on behalf of the coroner. In a small number of cases police may be required to be physically present and witness the procedure at the morgue. Warren and some other police officers were at the morgue to become familiar with the procedure as part of their training.

The pathologist was cutting open a dead man's chest to reveal a blackened lung. To which all the police officers responded in unison, "Smoker!" To their surprise, the pathologist replied, "No. City dweller."

I was shocked to hear this and all I could think about was my little girls' lungs. I responded, "So, are you saying that every person who lives in a city has a blackened lung from the road debris, dust and pollutants?" Warren responded dryly "Yes."

How did it all work out? Well, we decided to move. But we changed our minds about moving to Hawaii as the liberal gun laws in America conflicted with our values. We couldn't bring ourselves to take our daughters where 50 people die each year from guns. Now while 50 deaths a year from guns doesn't sound like many, it's a completely different number when one of those fatalities includes your child.

Instead, we moved to the Sapphire Coast of New South Wales. Though it took us another move to Camberwell, out in the burbs and away from the city. And four years of planning and restructuring our business, and our lives to make our final move.

We now live five minutes from pristine, sapphire ocean. We enjoy fresh air and friendly people (without guns). We have a huge vegetable garden and our whole family is the healthiest we've ever been.

On January 1 each year, I invest time on the first morning of my new year to consider my personal and my family's needs for the year.

Something that I would like to share though. It amazed me how much we all coughed on moving here. It was like our lungs were releasing the city dweller drudge. Now, when we travel to a city, we can smell the polluted air quality. Something we had no awareness of while living among it.

So, that's my big reason for putting on your oxygen mask first. Let me know share how you can do that too.

My diary helps me to plan and I'm always mindful to keep me in the plan too. Not just all I have to do. It's surprising sometimes how we put everyone else ahead of ourselves. So, I now have a new ritual that helps to consider my needs.

Since 2012, after moving to the Sapphire Coast, here's what I do.

On the first of January each year, I invest an hour of my time, on the first morning of my new year, to consider my personal needs and my family's needs for the year.

I sit down in my office, usually in shorts and a T shirt, because it's normally one of those warm summer days that time of year and I love having holidays at home around Christmas.

> **Putting yourself in your diary first is about saving your soul.**

I like to take around eight weeks off at that time because I've been coaching and teaching all year. Frankly, I'm exhausted from helping people and solving problems. Most evenings after coaching, I'm still thinking about my clients and how they can reach their goals or overcome their issues. It can be hard to switch off sometimes. So, Christmastime is bliss for me.

When it's holiday time, it's an excellent time to consider, "What does R!k need and want?" While I'm at it, "What does our family need and want?"

Before the end of the year, our family has a dinner to talk about our needs for the next calendar year. So, I start doodling away some of our ideas on a notepad. Then we discuss these at length with my wife Rebecca and my daughters Zoe and Sienna.

Then I come back into my office with our list of needs and wants. Can you guess what I do next?

Yep! You got it. I start putting those tasks, actions and events in my diary. That means we plan our holidays in advance, and we get the best deals. Once we decide where we are going, my wife Rebecca gets busy on finding the best places to stay and gets the best prices. It's amazing how much you save when you plan ahead.

But the point I'm trying to make here is not about saving money. It's about saving your soul. It's putting yourself in your diary first. It's putting on your oxygen mask before others.

Way before we start planning training dates and what days we're doing what for *Life Beyond Limits*. We're putting our family first.

It's amazing how your diary fills up with appointments that are for the benefit of clients and customers. That's a key catalyst to burnout. How do I know this? Well, the clients who come to me to help them through burnout don't get coaching to remedy the cause of burnout. They're getting coaching on the symptoms of burnout! In other words, they're already burnt out!

One thing that is common among all my burnout clients is this. None of them plan their diary with themselves in mind. They fill their diaries with tasks and take whatever is left, if anything for themselves. They have no real control of their lives. Either their company or business controls them. In some cases, their family controls them too.

I recall a client who came to me to get help to move beyond his depression. I'd worked with his wife who also had depression and she responded well to my program.

We sat there in a session. I was about to go through my usual process when an idea came to me loud and strong, and I ran with it.

I asked my client to consider all the things that he loved to do and to say them out loud so I could write them all down. He started to list them. 'Fishing. Going for a picnic with his family. Doing up old cars. Going camping. Sitting with friends around a campfire.' The list went on and I kept writing.

"When was the last time you did any of these things?" I asked him, as I repeated the list back to him. I could tell by his eyes moving into the visual remembered quadrant that he hadn't done any of these things for quite some time.

Then I asked him to rate each of the things on his list from zero to ten. Zero were things he didn't like at all, right up to ten. These were the things he loved the most and everything else was somewhere in-between. While he never gave any one of them a ten, he was an Australian after all, and Australian's don't like to rate anything with a ten. There's always got to be room to move and improve. So, there were a few eights and the odd nine.

My next instruction was simple but took a little planning. I asked him to put into his diary all the eights and nines. Which he did. In just a few weeks his depression was gone.

So, here's the lesson, just in case you missed it. Put yourself in your diary first.

TIME SAVERS AND TIMELY QUESTIONS

1. Put yourself in your diary first.

2. Before the end of the year, sit down with your partner or family or yourself and consider your needs for the next calendar year. Doodle away some ideas on a notepad.
3. On the first of January each year, invest an hour of your time and put your personal needs in your diary, before anything else goes in there.

9. Bending Time

A little Soul once asked the Maker a question. One that I'm sure we all would love to know the answer to. The question it asked was short, but deep, "Why am I in this body, living this life?"

The Maker answered, "We'll that's entirely up to you. You can choose to learn to live or you can live to learn?" He continued, "You chose your body and your life to learn your soul's lessons."

The little soul confused, needed clarity, "So, if I chose to live and learn, what am I living for and what am I here to learn?"

The Maker gleefully responded, "You are here to live your purpose and your earth's assignment is learn enough to live it."

"But what if I have found my purpose and I am living it?" the little Soul responded.

The Maker smiled, "Then time for you will not drag for eternity. Once you have learned enough to live your purpose, time will move much faster for you and soon you will return home."

Time is not the same for everyone. Time is a distortion. As a coach who has helped numerous people to move through depression, anxiety and trauma, I can attest that for them, time slows down. It dra-a-a-a-a-g-s. Yet once they are relieved of the causes of their symptoms and we do some helpful brain untraining, time again speeds up for them.

Let me show this to you if you'll allow me to.

Think back to a time in the past. A nice time that you can recall easily. The first nice time that springs to mind will do. Relax and close your eyes for a moment if this makes it much easier? Yes, you're going to have to put down this book for a moment to make this work.

**Time is measured by our emotions
more than by our watches or clocks.**

Now, ask yourself; How much time did you invest to recall this experience? And how much time did you invest to have the original experience?

How long did it take to experience the event? How long did it take to travel there (if you did travel that is)? How long did it take to prepare?

Though how quickly were you able to experience that feeling again?

When you consider the nice feeling that you felt recalling the memory, the time and money you invested, the preparation, the travel to the original event seems less important.

I hope you just had a light-globe go off or a little heart flutter. Because if you did, you would realise that time is not measured by time. Time is so often measured by our emotions more than by our watches or clocks.

The way you experienced time in that little exercise relates to Einstein's 'Law of Relativity.' You remember Einstein's 'Law Of Relatively' don't you?

In case you need the refresher, let me explain it for you. I won't go as far as explaining $E=MC^2$ but I'll outline the two fundamental concepts that lead there. Though stay with me, as this is likely to get a little heady.

The first thing to know is that motion cannot be proven. Time can't even be validated by science, as much as they may try.

Absolute motion is the idea that a thing can't be said to be moving, with no frame of reference whatsoever.

In other words, picture yourself floating in a never-ending white space. All you can see is you. You can't see anyone else and nothing else. You cannot see any corners or distinctive factors. If you moved, such as you walked, you wouldn't be able to prove with any certainty if you were moving forwards or not. You have nothing to reference your rate of movement against.

The only way you would know you were moving is if a second thing existed that wasn't moving. At least not at the same pace as you. The other object allows you to tell if you are moving further away from the second thing or getting closer to it or if you are parallel to it.

For example, if a floor or ceiling existed and your feet or head touched them, that would be a frame of reference. You now have two things that exist, and one determines the other as a reference point. Are you still with me?

So, Einstein's first axiom shows that all motion is relative.

The second axiom: The speed of light is constant.

To say the speed of light is constant sounds unremarkable at first. It states that light always travels at the same speed. Once we start considering what it means though, some incredible consequences emerge.

The speed of light is 299,792,458 metres per second. To make this a little easier, let's refer to it as 300,000 km per second. It's a nice round number Yet, it's an unfathomably big number that is difficult to get your head around. To put it into perspective, if you could travel at the speed of light, you could circle the Earth over seven times in a single second. You could reach the moon in 1.3 seconds and in 3 minutes you'd be on Mars, and in a mere 8.20 minutes you'd be on the sun. It would be a tad hot on your toes, but you will have made it there all the same.

Now let us get a bit weirder. Perhaps frizzle your hair like Einstein or let the physics do it for you? That's of course if you have hair—unlike me.

The speed of light (in a vacuum) does not accelerate nor decelerate. It always travels at a constant speed known as 'C,' otherwise known as the 'cosmic speed limit'. So, the speed of light must remain constant for all observers. It doesn't change or alter for anyone.

To say that the speed of light is the same for all observers, regardless of how fast the observer is travelling, is to say that if you were standing still, light would be travelling away from you at 300,000km/s.

It also says that if you were travelling at 100 kph, light would still be travelling away from you at 300,000 km/s.

If you could strangely find some way to travel at 100,000 kph, light would still be travelling away from you at 300,000 km/s.

How is this even possible?

We get the measure for speed by dividing distance by time. You take the distance you have travelled and divide it by the time it took you to get there. If you travelled 120 kilometres and it took you 2 hours, you travelled at 60 kilometres per hour (120/2=60). It's confusing, I know. It did my head in too. Though let's bring this to some level of simplicity, because when you get that time is relative, you'll get more time.

Time is malleable and technically everyone has their own measure of it.

Einstein discovered that just like motion, time is not an absolute concept. Time is malleable and technically everyone has their own measure of it. Okay, if you still don't get it. This will help.

Professor Einstein's secretary was so burdened with inquiries about the meaning of 'relativity' that the professor decided to help her out. He explained it simply and brilliantly. "When you sit with a nice girl for two hours, to you it's only a minute, but when you sit on a hot stove for a minute, you think it's two hours. That's relativity."

Let me make it even simpler for you. Time can only be measured by the observer and the observer of your own time is you. But now that you know that you have another question.

If you measure your own time, how do *you* measure it?

**"When you get your head around how time bends, you will have people bending over backwards for your time"
– R!k Schnabel**

While others may measure time by the number of tasks completed or money earned.

You measure it by the quality of your feelings. The better you feel, the greater the quality of time. But the better you feel, the faster time flies. That's relativity.

I recall a time that I was at a party with a lady. We were sitting on cushions on the floor, just mere inches apart. We were deep in conversation and while there were many people all around us. But you know what? They all disappeared for me. I could only see the lady in front of me and she is the only person I heard. I couldn't hear anyone else. It was the time that I first said, "I love you" to my wife.

When you measure time by the quality of your feelings, you increase your value of time.

Now I cannot tell you how long that duration of time was. I have no idea. But I can say that it seemed to go in a flash. Though the feelings that remain in my heart about that time is highly valuable to me because it felt so good. At time of writing, we have been married for 21 years, yet that time flew.

Hence, when you measure time by the quality of your feelings, and you aim to create great feelings, you increase your value of time.

It raises an interesting question.

What would your life look like, if you stopped measuring your life by your years of life? What would it sound like if you measured time by the quality of your connections? What if you measured your life by the quality of your feelings? Would it change how you saw your world? Would it change how you hear the world? Would it change how you felt the world and your life? More importantly, would it change your day-to-day decisions?

The truth is that time is an illusion. Let me prove it you in the next chapter.

TIME SAVERS AND TIMELY QUESTIONS

1. Plan to put valuable feelings into your time.
2. What would your life look like, if you stopped measuring your life by your years of life? What would it sound like if you measured time by the quality of your connections or the joy in your heart?

10. Is Time An Illusion?

We are master storytellers. We tell ourselves fanciful stories to motivate ourselves to get vast amounts of work done in small amounts of time. We jot down task after task after task, sure that we can complete them all within a standard workday. And yet, at the end of the day, we're stunned to find that our work remains unfinished. Then we have to dash to the finish line.

We're not deliberately deceiving ourselves about what we can do with our time. But despite past evidence, in the moment we're convinced we'll be able to achieve the extraordinary in an ordinary day.

This is called 'magical thinking,' and it can cause you to disappoint others, miss deadlines, feel depleted, and lose your inspiration.

In my book, "**7 Beliefs That Will Change Your Life**"[1] I suggested that 'Time is an illusion.' Time confuses us at every opportunity. The clock seems to sneakily speed up and slow down, depending upon how we observe time. What do I mean by observe? The way we experience time and watch time.

We of course know that the moment we decide to watch time, like the idiom, a watched pot never boils, time moves at snail's pace. It takes for-e--v---e----r.

As a child, you may recall how long the time dragged to get to Christmas or your birthday. Though the moment they arrived, time shot past you like a bullet. This explains why time moves slowly for people who wait for things to happen—and races for more action-orientated people. It's true. Time moves faster for active people. People who pack more into their lives. Particularly if they are passionate or enjoying their experiences of life.

We humans measure time in units. Time is seconds to minutes, hours to days, days to weeks, months to years and decades to eons. This suggests that time is linear and each specific unit of time is exactly the same. Time, my friend, is not linear at all. Yet, the illusion of our measuring devices would have us believe so. Time is relative, exactly as Einstein theorised. Time changes depending upon the meaning we place upon it.

In *The Neuroscience of Leadership* David Rock and Jeffrey Schwartz explained the altering of time. Neurons communicate with each other through a type of electrochemical signalling that is driven by the movement of ions such as sodium, potassium, and calcium. These ions travel through channels within the brain that are, at their narrowest point, only a little more than a single ion wide. This means that the brain is a quantum environment and is therefore subject to all the surprising laws of quantum mechanics. One of these laws is the Quantum Zeno Effect (QZE). The QZE was described in 1977 by the physicist George Sudarshan at the *University of Texas* at Austin and was verified many times since.

Thinking alters with time and time alters with thinking.

The QZE is related to the established observer effect of quantum physics: The behaviour and position of any atom-sized entity, such as an atom, an electron, or an ion, appears to change when the entity is observed. In the QZE, when any system is observed in a sufficiently rapid, repetitive fashion, the rate at which that system changes is reduced. In quantum physics, as in the rest of life, a watched pot never boils.[2]

Though you can be excused for not being able to understand such scientific rhetoric.

It is much easier for us to think in linear terms than it is to understand the world of quantum physics. It's not as easy as one plus one equals two, or is it?

One plus one equals two because someone created it, made it so, sold it and we bought it.

We are not completely clear who created the modern number system we use today. Although called Arabic numerals because it came to Europe through the Arabs, the Arabs themselves call it 'HindSaa' meaning — given by Hindus or Indians.

But where did the Arabs get numerals from?

The Persians copied the Indian number system and then passed it on to the Arabs. Then Fibonacci, an Italian mathematician travelled to Algeria to study. When he came back home, he brought the Indian numerals with him. He wrote about the system in his book Liber Abaci. This system soon gained wide acceptance throughout Europe.[3]

Today this is the number system used by practically the whole world. A large majority of the population now believes that one plus one does in fact equal two, though most entrepreneurs have another formula. Entrepreneurs believe that one plus one equals at least four! They believe that one action can cause a multi-result; they call it — leverage. One person doubles (at least) their efficiency and that of another, equalling at least four. This is what it means when you hear, 'two heads are better than one.'

Leverage has the power to completely alter what is possible in a duration of time. Let us say that one skilled carpenter can build one table in one day. Yet, one entrepreneur can have that same carpenter teach ten others how to build a table. We can now produce eleven tables in one day. The same time, the same effort, but a completely different result. The power of leverage's multiplier effect.

While it is easier to think in linear terms, at times, our linear thinking creates problems in our mind with one plus one rational; let me elaborate.

There was a time in my life when I held a belief: I don't have enough money. It was real for me as it was true or at least I thought it was true because the evidence was there.

Linear problems will not go away with linear thinking.

After working for 12 months in a new sales career in Melbourne, Australia, I was $35,000 in debt and only had $27 in the bank to show for all my work. I believed I was the worst salesperson on the planet, and I would continue to lose money. Linear thinking would have me assume that in twelve more months my debt would grow, or I would be broke. Perhaps I would be $70,000 in debt, unless of course I changed part of the formula. Linear problems will not go away with linear thinking.

I decided to embrace some extraordinary thinking. I let go of one plus one equals two, this equals that. At the time, my friends thought I was crazy when I decided to invest almost $35,000 in learning Life Coaching and Neuro Linguistic Programming (NLP). Few of them had ever invested in self-education and in their minds, this did not solve my problem, it just put me deeper in debt. I knew that NLP helped people to turn their thinking around and what I needed was a complete turnaround! The result was that learning NLP seemed to accelerate time itself!

Making more money in less time was previously outside of my beliefs. During my NLP training, a fellow student in my class helped me to change a terrible, limiting belief. This shift resulted in me earning two years income in just 3 weeks!

Now I know that might sound incredibly bizarre or perhaps it doesn't even stack up mathematically. Though I discovered that you could change just one belief and life does a quantum leap on you. Not only did my training completely fix my problem. I became an accredited Life Coach and a Life Coach Trainer. I decided to continue training until I attained my Trainer qualification, so I could teach accredited level NLP, Life Coaching and Ericksonian Hypnotherapy.

I now had new skills, new thinking and new money. This one extraordinary decision changed my entire life. It is the very reason you're reading this book right now. I mastered not only how to change my beliefs, I seemed to master time itself.

To change my financial future, present and past, I learned to release the pain and emotional anguish I held around money. I made peace with my childhood at being refused pocket money. I made peace with every moment I compared myself to successful people and stopped looking down at myself and judging myself harshly.

Then I discovered more beliefs that were creating my previous poor outcomes. I changed:

My poor beliefs.

My I'm doing it tough beliefs.

The I'm not worthy of keeping my money beliefs.

My I haven't got enough time beliefs, and

I'm not a leader beliefs, among many others.

I'm sure we both know of people who believe they can and so make the average persons' annual income in weeks. Some do that in days or even minutes. While we all have the same time available to us, some people's beliefs will have them create fortunes. Beliefs alone will alter time.

Our beliefs at times, are the thin line that separates failure from success. Beliefs divide obscurity from stardom and rags from riches. It is like two people can be on the same planet but on two completely different wave lengths or two different planes of time. So, let's get back to time and view it from a completely different perspective.

Japanese females are expected to live to 86. Yet, if you were female and lived in a small republic in Africa, the Republic of Sierra Leone, you could only expect to live to 47. According to United Nations World Population Prospects Worldwide, the average life expectancy at birth was 67.88 years (65.71 years for males and 70.14 years for females) over the period 2005–2010.[4]

If we take the average life expectancy of 67.88 years and round that number up to 68, let's look at time in another way.

We can look at time in years, months, weeks, days, minutes, seconds and even microseconds! Though if we examine 68 years in a different unit of time, time seems to alter. At birth with 68 years' worth of life left, you start with approximately 3,536 weeks or 24,752 days or 594,048 hours, 35,642,880 minutes, or 2,138,572,800 seconds.

Now let's work with minutes as I'm sure we could achieve a lot with almost 36 million minutes. When I first wrote this particular chapter from my book, '7 Beliefs That Will Change Your Life,' it was ten years ago. I was 51 years old. I realised I had less than 36 million minutes remaining.

Based on an average life span and my current age in years and months, I only had 8,539,200 more minutes to live, and while that might seem like a big number to you, a minute will pass quickly. In fact, when I first wrote this chapter, I had 8,539,200 minutes. Now as upon my final edit before this goes to my publisher, that number has reduced to 8,272,800. In that time, 266,400 minutes have elapsed! Every day that passes, we lose 1,440 minutes — so I'm guessing I better get on with it.

How many years do you have left to live?

When we view our life in minutes it changes our perspective of time. While my eight million or so minutes might seem like a big number, the rapid rate that a minute flies by makes the end of my life seem more imminent than the 6 years I now have left. (Well, I think I'll live longer than that because I'm far from average! They're my beliefs anyway). Though who knows, I might have died by the time you read this? I hope my time invested here was worth it for you.

What would happen to your productivity if you were paid by the minute instead of by the hour? Lawyers for example charge in 6-minute blocks while accountants charge per hour. Who values their time more? Who earns more?

If we view our life in years, we will perhaps not value the hours or minutes that pass us by. Let's focus on you now...

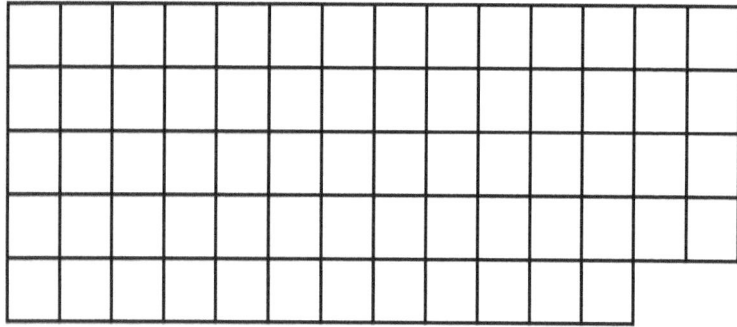

If you completed this formula, you'll get an idea of how many minutes you have left (I've omitted leap years to keep the formula simple).

68 years –_____ your age = _____ years x 525,600 minutes = _____ minutes left.

When we look at time that we have left visually, it again can seem quite different. In the grid above, there are 68 squares representing an average life in years. Shade off some boxes to make up your current age. In other words, if you're 30 years old, shade off 30 boxes (starting from top left) so you can see how much life you have left (by average life expectancy of course).

If you're like me, with eight or so million minutes left, what does that feel like to you? How does this alter your thinking about life? How does it cause you to think about your productivity or does it stir the concept of a legacy?

Do you have any plans about what you will leave your family or the world in your lifetime? And how much time do you have left to create or build that legacy? While even one million minutes might seem a lot, each minute that passes equates to a minute that is gone forever. Chances are by the time you've read this chapter, 25 or so of your minutes will have vanished forever. By the end of today another 1,440 minutes will be gone. Eventually like me, your time will be up.

You might only be a memory. Perhaps remembered for how much you valued your time or what legacy you left while here on earth. Maybe you shall be remembered for what you did or didn't do while you were here. Now that we put context to time, it again changes time itself.

When Einstein's lifelong friend Besso's 35 million minutes were up. Einstein wrote a letter to Besso's family, saying "…that although Besso had preceded him in death it was of no consequence, for us physicists believe the separation between past, present, and future is only an illusion, although a convincing one."

Einstein proved that time is relative, not absolute as Newton once claimed. Einstein believed that with the proper technology, such as a fast rocket ship, the person in the rocket will experience several days while another person on the ground, moving at the speed of the rotation of the earth, simultaneously experiences only a few hours or minutes. The same two people can meet up again, one having experienced days or even years while the other has only experienced minutes. The person in the rocket only needs to travel near to the speed of light to distort time. The faster they travel, the slower their time will pass relative to someone planted firmly on the earth. If they were able to travel at the speed of light, their time would cease completely, and they would only exist trapped in timelessness.

If you've ever been in a car or motorbike accident at high speed, you will have experienced Einstein's theory of relativity.

I recall being in a high-speed accident on a motorbike. My front wheel slipped out from under me and while the accident took only five or so seconds to conclude, it didn't feel like that at all. While I wasn't travelling anywhere close to the speed of light (officer), I recall every second as if it were minutes. As I mentally recall the accident, it seems as though it lasted at least two minutes.

Conversely, can you recall an entire joyous holiday that lasted days or weeks? My guess is that the holiday felt like it was over in a flash! That is what Einstein called relativity. Time is relative to the observer and the value of time is dependent upon what you do with it. Leonardo Da Vinci said, "Time stays long enough for those who use it."

**Your time is valued by the duration
and intensity of your focus.**

With over eight billion people on the planet today, the next hour will be experienced radically different by almost everyone. It seems that what we believe about time is entirely different depending upon who we are, what is going on in our life at the time, and how old or young we are.

The irony is that older people seem to take their time while they have less of it, while teenagers sometimes act like there's no tomorrow. The issue is not how much time we have or haven't, the issue is what we're focusing on and how long we can hold our focus! So, you could say that your time is valued by the duration and intensity of your focus.

Wherever you place your focus determines how you experience time. The power of focus is the power of life. If you can focus on a solution, then you'll surely nail it.

If you focus on the problem, it is likely you'll keep the problem, and the problem might even get bigger or worse.

Neurons that fire together, wire together.

When we have problems, time seems to drag on forever. This follows the principle of 'Where your focus goes, energy flows.' Energy alters time. Get motivated, get energised, get ferociously focused and time will become insignificant. The irony of life is the more passionate and energetic you are, the faster life seems to evaporate.

When we concentrate our attention upon a specific experience, we light up associated neural pathways in our brain. Whether through a thought, a picture in our mind, an insight or an emotional situation or fear, this maintains the brain's neural pathways. It keeps the thought alive.

Concentration holds that state in association with the experience. Paying enough attention to any specific brain connection keeps the relevant circuitry open and dynamically alive. These circuits can then eventually become not just chemical links but stable, physical changes in the brain's structure. In my work, we have a saying, 'Neurons that fire together, wire together.'

Cognitive scientists have known for 30 years that the brain is capable of significant internal changes in response to environmental changes. A dramatic finding when it was first made. We now also know that the brain changes as a function of where an individual puts his or her attention. The power is in the focus.

People who practice a specialty every day literally think differently. In business, professionals in different functions; finance, operations, legal, research and development, marketing, design, and human resources, have physiological differences that prevent them from seeing the world and time in the same way.

This explains why my training company is often called into organisations to help them to work together in a more harmonious way.

> **Poor people value money over time.**
> **Rich people value their time over money.**

I recall a media company where the sales team could not work together with the editorial team because both believed they were working for a different cause. Essentially, it's what we call a 'values conflict.' However, when they worked together, it made everyone's lives easier. The company's profits increased and the company agreed to incentivise both departments. A small investment in time and resources with a big and harmonious upside.

To gain mastery of your life, is to be the master of your beliefs and your time. Develop convenient beliefs and focus on what you do want, and not on what you don't want.

Here are the two beliefs we mentioned earlier that limit people's lives.

Belief #1 — I don't have enough money, and

Belief #2 — I don't have enough time.

These two beliefs can be the perfect recipe for failure. After years of wealth coaching, the distinction I have on the subject is those who value their time will typically make more money. The longer you sustain your focus on wealth, the more wealth you will likely acquire.

It seems to me that too many people these days look for the fast buck and as a result seldom succeed. These days I run from anyone who uses the words, fast and money in the same sentence.

Time is a conundrum as is wealth. Most people get these mixed up when aiming to grow their wealth. For example: poor people value money over time. They will give away their days, their months and their years of life for money and perhaps a gold watch.

Wealthy people value time over money. They know that their time is precious. Well invested time can make all the difference. What most people make in a month, they can make in a day, perhaps even minutes. The reason? Wealthy people will often invest more time to build their networks, go deeper into study and invest in their thinking.

The fascinating thing I've observed with money, is the more you have, the more you value your time. Poor people will ask, "What's my annual income?" while wealthy people will ask, "Is it worth my time?" or "Is there a better place to invest my time?"

Expand your vision ten or twenty years into the future, instead of just focusing on tomorrow or yesterday. The best time strategy in my mind is to plan for the future and be conscious enough to act in the present. Perhaps you could even have a vision to create a legacy and extend your vision to a thousand years! What would your time look like if you were to build something of value that was to be appreciated for the next thousand years? Would you value time differently?

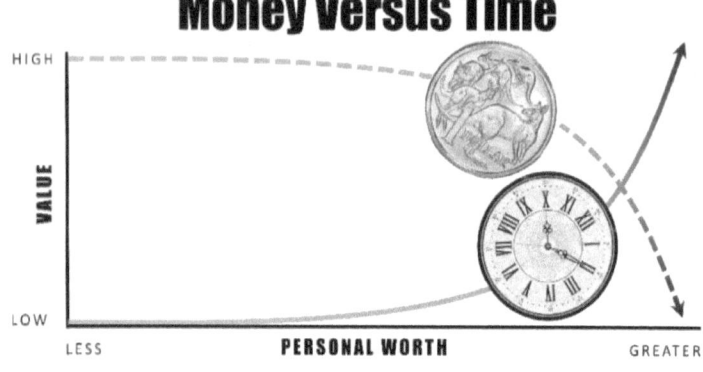

People for whom time moves quickly are usually focused on creating their lives as if every minute counts! While for others who have little or no focus, time will seem to drag. Create a vision and time becomes a well assigned asset. Create no vision and you will more likely squander time.

One final thing about improving the value of time, you might find this useful. While the average person may have 595,680 hours available to them, most people will be sleeping for 198,560 of them or for 8,273 days. If you got up just one hour earlier or went to bed one hour later each day, you would have another 24,820 hours available to you. It was never about time; was it? It's more about focus and commitment; isn't it?

I use healing audio programs while I sleep to create my night-time University — you can download some here: https://lifebeyondlimits.com.au/healing-audios/

We cannot manage time; we can only plan our time and manage ourselves within it.

So, what's really, really important to you? Make it happen in this lifetime by valuing this second and making a decision to start now! Go ahead, put down this book and take one step forward on an idea. You can read the next chapter tomorrow.

TIME SAVERS AND TIMELY QUESTIONS

1. How many more years do you have left based on the average age of 68?
2. Will you plan your time by what you will achieve in a year? A month? A week? An hour? A minute?
3. If you were to leave a legacy, what would you leave to the world or your family?
4. Do you really not have enough time or do you not have enough focus?
5. Do you really not have enough money or do you not have enough creativity?

11. Turn Distraction To Action

A Master was sharing with his student the reasons why distractions weaken even the strongest of us. Leaning forward he said, "Most courageous lion tamers use two tools to control and 'tame' their fierce companions who prowl around the cage. A whip and a stool, or a chair." Then he asked his student, "Which of the two is the most valuable to the tamer?"

The student replied, "Surely the whip."

The Master responded abruptly, "No. The one most important tool is the stool, and more specifically, the four legs of the stool!"

Reflectively, the student replied, "That's odd! Why so?"

The Master continued, "A lion can overpower, maul and kill a person. Yet, it's only easy for the lion to do so if it can focus on the singular object of the person. The lion tamer uses the stool as a method of distraction. When faced with the legs of the stool, the lion tries to focus on all four at once. Confused, and unable to focus, it stands there, frozen! The strength of the lion is weakened, and the lion tamer remains safe behind the stool."

**Ninety-five percent of thought, emotion and learning occur in the unconscious mind
– that is, without our awareness.**

Like a lion being tamed, did you know that we are hypnotised for much of our day? A boring conversation will do it. Scrolling on social media will definitely do it. On average, within seven seconds of sitting in front of the television your children are hypnotised and you're not far behind.[1]

The next time you see a young boy or girl on the roof adorning a tea towel like a cape, you know what is about to unfold. If images of Superman or Superwoman are entering your mind right now, you immediately get a sense of the power of TV.

What! Did you think you made conscious choices? Think again.

Harvard Professor, Gerald Zaltman suggests that "Ninety-five percent of thought, emotion and learning occur in the unconscious mind—that is, without our awareness."[2]

> **The average employee wastes up to 41% of their time at work on low-value tasks.**

Do you think that we're remarkably able to concentrate undistracted for long periods of time? The plain truth is we are ruled by our unconscious mind. Our unconscious minds are emotionally driven and easily distracted.

So, it shouldn't shock you at all to learn that today's knowledge workers are notoriously distracted. In fact, researchers have extensively studied the topic. Still, the stats are startling:

> **If we learned to manage our communication technology in a more efficient manner, we could give the economy a $900 million to $1.3 trillion boost per year.**

The average employee wastes up to 41% of their time at work on low-value tasks.

53% of employees waste at least one hour every day dealing with distractions.

Slack's average user sends 200 messages every day.

The average worker spends 1 hour and 5 minutes of their workday reading news sites.

Social media takes up 44 minutes of the average worker's day.[3]

Then when we do start doing real work, we're rarely able to concentrate. Work from Gloria Mark at the *University of California, Irvine* has shown that workers typically attend to a task for about three minutes before switching to something else (usually an electronic communication). A recent study found that a typical employee only has 11 minutes between distractions. Other studies show that office workers are interrupted about seven times an hour, which adds up to 56 interruptions a day, 80% of which are considered trivial.

According to *McKinsey & Company*, high-skilled workers spend a staggering 28% of their working hours reading and replying to e-mail messages.

If we learned to manage our communication technology in a more efficient manner, we could give the economy a $900 million to $1.3 trillion boost per year.

Social media costs the U.S. economy $650 billion every year.

When you find yourself sitting in the office feeling bored or overwhelmed, it's easy to automatically check your social media. But it comes at a high price. Social media costs the U.S. economy $650 billion every year.[4]

Not only are distractions frequent, but they kill productivity. Even brief mental blocks created by shifting between tasks can cost as much as 40% of your productive time. This is due to a phenomenon called 'attention residue.' Research shows that when you switch tasks it takes a long time to get back to the level of efficiency you were at before you were interrupted.

"People need to stop thinking about one task in order to fully transition their attention and perform well on another," Researcher Sophie Leroy wrote. "Yet, results indicate it is difficult for people to transition their attention away from an unfinished task and their subsequent task performance suffers."

The problem with interruptions is that it takes 25 minutes and 26 seconds on average to get back on track. Other studies put it at 23 minutes. Either way, it's easy to see how a workday can flash before our eyes all while our to-do list looks the same at the end of the day as it did that morning.

Deep work is the most productive work.

Productivity gurus including Cal Newport and Nir Eyal argue that deep, profitable work requires chunks of uninterrupted time that are at least two hours, preferably longer. Chunks shorter than two hours impose unnecessary switching costs.

When Newport looked at profiles of 25 famously prolific, creative people, he found they spent an average of 5.25 hours per day in deep work. Most of us, Newport argues in Deep Work, have about four hours of deep work in us per day. Newport himself works two 2–3-hour chunks per day.

It's in those focus time periods that most workers get most of their real work done.

For example, in Deep Work, Cal Newport describes how Carl Jung wrote his books in a tower with no electricity to minimize distraction. Mark Twain wrote much of The Adventures of Tom Sawyer in a shed in New York so far from his family they blew a horn at mealtimes. Theoretical Physicist Peter Higgs, the namesake of the Higgs boson particle, has never sent an email, surfed the internet, or used a mobile phone. He was so out of touch that journalists couldn't contact him to tell him he'd won a Nobel Prize.

Due to the many distractions that kept me from writing my first book, I booked a cabin by the ocean and in just days it was finished.

A productive question that you might be asking yourself right now is, "What has to go in order for productivity to increase?" Or perhaps, "Where do I have to go to double-down my productivity?"

TIME SAVERS AND TIMELY QUESTIONS

1. Create 2-hour chunks of time to do productive deep work.
2. Ask yourself, "What has to go in order for productivity to increase?" Or perhaps, "Where do I have to go to double-down my productivity?"
3. Limit your TV viewing.

12. Systemise To Save Time

Some systems serve us but systems out of context, do not serve us at all. One day I headed into a liquor store. Coming from inside the store, a colonel came out carrying two bags. I couldn't help it. My sense of humour got the better of me and I snapped to attention and saluted. The colonel responded in kind. Then we both heard it. The soul-crunching sound of both bags crashing to the pavement. As the colonel's liquor seeped into the gutter, he choked out, "Don't ever salute me again!" He was so entrained to salute that he couldn't stop himself. Imagine if you could do that with your time and focus. Anyone can do it. Just start a habit.

My colleagues are often befuddled by all I am able to get done in my day. Some have called me an enigma. From the outside I may appear complex but from the inside, from where I stand, I am a fan of simplicity.

Can I share a system with you that helps my clients solve problems and reach their goals with ease? It's also how I increase my own productivity and that of my clients.

The key strategy I use to get so many things done is the same strategy I teach my coach and therapist

students. In our *Master Coach + NLP Master Practitioner Training*[1] I have added training modules which I call the 'Coaching Series." This is where I ask for a volunteer from among our students and I coach them from beginning to resolution. This is so our students can experience many coaching sessions to watch and hear how it's done.

I commence these sessions by explaining that clients often present their issues and goals like a bowl of spaghetti. Their issues and goals are an entangled mess of beginnings, middles and ends. It's a mish mash of events, a litany of she saids and he saids, and a quandary of emotions.

Systems are a process that delivers the outcomes that people trust. Without systems you cannot trust that a valuable prize will be attained.

Our job as a coach is to dig through the spaghetti. To find where to start and to discover how to end the saga or reach the goal. Now, I can tell you that speed of solution will not come from a barrage of random questions that coaches favour. You need systemise because your systems will save you and your client's precious time.

Solving people's complex problems, helping to get my clients clear I learned from my many teachers and mentors, and from some of my own coaches. Though how I systematically and speedily resolve my clients' issues was never taught to me. These came to me from over 20 years of coaching, now exceeding 38,000 hours of face-to-face change work. I believe my systems and the speed of resolution that they give me are my je ne sais quoi. It's the reason I get so may referrals and why my clients gladly pay my fees.

> **I believe true talent comes over time and once you know what the 'key drivers' to talent are, and you focus on them, you soon develop speed.**

It always reminds me of the story about the woman who approached Picasso in a restaurant. Knowing his famed reputation, she asked him to scribble something on a napkin. Flippantly, she said she would be happy to pay whatever he felt it was worth. Picasso complied and then said, "That will be $10,000."

"But you did that in thirty seconds," the astonished woman replied.

"No," Picasso said. "It has taken me forty years to do that."

I believe true talent comes over time and once you know what the 'key drivers' to talent are, and you focus on them, you soon develop speed.

Systems are a process that delivers the outcomes that people trust. Without systems you cannot trust that a valuable prize will be attained.

> **Passionate people produce more than fearful people. People who worry about competition and loss of income usually have their beliefs confirmed.**

My students say I'm a generous trainer, though I would say that I'm a passionate trainer and I'm passionately unrelenting when it comes to coaching. I want my students to have my best. My colleagues ask, "Why are you such a fool for teaching your students how to be as good as you are. Aren't you creating more competition for yourself?" I usually respond with, "Why don't you ask a better question?" These people do not realise that passionate people produce more than fearful people. People who worry about competition and loss of income usually have their beliefs confirmed.

Now. Back to my clients and their bowls of spaghetti. How do you get through all of that mess? One word, and you know what that word is: systems.

GASM stands for my Goals, Actions, Strategies and Measures system.

A system I invented to help my clients is called 'GASM.' Yes, I know what you're thinking! My students got there before you. When I ask, "How do you get a result for your clients?" They respond, "You can find your way or GASM." Our little joke.

Let me share a quick story where I believe GASM originated.

In our training programs, we often attract trained psychologists. They enrol because they wish to complement their practice by studying my methods. One delightful female psychologist, a practised therapist for over 30 years once came up to me in class one day. She said, "I've worked out your philosophy that underpins your methodology." I was curious to hear her revelation.

She continued, "In psychology we're taught to assess our patients and our diagnosis tells us which box to put them in. Then of course we put in that box whatever is needed.

Your methodology holds one philosophy that is key to your success." She paused for effect and my attention.

"According to you, there is no box. You have one goal in mind and that is to not focus on the symptom, but on the solution—as there must be one."

I thanked her then and I must thank her again now, as I believe that conversation led me to design GASM. So let me share it with you.

Let me show you how simple this system is to use by sharing a case history that was complex.

A client who came to see me some years ago said to me that she thought she was going insane. Let's call her Sandy. Let me warn you in advance, this story might be challenging for some to hear.

I like to start my coaching sessions by allowing my clients to share extensively as I take notes. My notes allow me to see words and phrases that eventually stand out like red beacons. I simplify the complexity of coaching by circling key words particularly.

Sandy told me that as a child, her mother would physically scold her without warning or cause. From age thirteen her mother earned an income from prostituting Sandy. Sandy's mother would lock her own daughter in a bedroom with friends and strangers.

After escaping the clutches of her mother, at 17 Sandy vanished out of her bedroom window and left home never to return. Homeless, she finally found work and rented a small apartment. For years Sandy saw therapist after therapist, without a resolution. She was now in her forties and her childhood trauma still haunted her.

A therapist suggested to Sandy that she knew someone who had a knack of solving complex problems and sent her to me.

Sandy's problematic symptom was extreme anger. She was easily triggered and while her husband was a patient man, her marriage hung by a thread.

In our first session she cried, she shouted and slammed her fists on the arms of her chair. I sat and watched every physical move and listened to every word. Trigger words started to appear, and I circled them.

Letting my clients talk allows us to build a connection and this builds trust. Trust is paramount in my business. As my clients start to trail off I thank them for their honesty and helping me to help them.

The first point in the GASM system is the G or the Goal. The goal is ultimately where we need to end, so it makes sense to make this our starting point.

I typically start the system with the GOAL by saying, "That's the problem but what is the goal or solution that you are needing? What is an ideal resolution for you?"

Now while a client is in a 'problem state' their neurological pathways are nowhere near a 'solution state.' In other words, it is difficult to see a positive outcome while in a negative state. However, the question sets a new direction. Once the goal is expressed, my next question leads to the ACTIONS.

"What have you tried? What actions have you taken to move beyond the problem?" To which Sandy explained she was just going around in circles. She continued to explain why she thought she was going insane. "How can a mother treat her own child so cruelly?" Besides the therapy Sandy had received, her only other action was to think. Thinking over and over, and over again in circles to seek to understand her mother's behaviour. Her actions gave me the answer that made Sandy sit silent for what seemed like minutes.

I said, "I get it. Sandy, you just told me at the very beginning that your problem was that you thought you were going insane. I now know why. You are trying to understand your mother's mind. A mind which could only be described as 'desperate' or 'insane.' The only way a rational mind could ever get close to understanding an insane mind is to become insane itself."

For the first time, Sandy's eyes changed from the fearful wide-eyed traumatised stares and anger filled furrowed brows to eyes that flashed from side to side. This new insight needed much processing.

Our sessions progressed well after that. We then built a series of STRATEGIES to craft a new way forward for Sandy. That's the S of GASM if you missed it. Here I like to brainstorm a pathway to my client's goal and finally ways in which we can MEASURE progress.

Of course, within the Strategies there was much therapeutic work. Processes and insights to help Sandy to remove the trauma. There was much brain untraining too. Untraining of all the abusive conditioning that perpetuated Sandy's anger and sadness. Though without a Goal there would be no direction. Without eliciting her past actions there would be no understanding. The strategies then provide a path forward and the measures allow us to calibrate her progress. Without GASM or perhaps another system, Sandy's life would have been a mirror of her past. Systems will save you time.

Just in case you missed it, GASM stands for Goals, Actions, Strategies and Measures.

> You too can get through so much more by building a system and following it—and of course, improving it as you go.

Taking the time to design systems may cost you time in the outset. Though systems will ultimately save you enormous time.

Henry Ford built more cars than any other car producer of his generation by building a system—the production line. You too can get through so much more by building a system and following it—and of course, improving it as you go.

I coach all sorts of people for all kinds of reasons and a desirable outcome is my goal. Where I see an opportunity to help, I'm usually sharing one of my systems or building one from scratch, using my logic and imagination.

When I hear that one of my clients is wasting their time answering emails, we'll usually design a system of templates. After-all, most of us get similar enquiries day after day and systemised templates or Frequently Asked Questions (FAQs) speed up responses.

Feel free to use GASM. Ask yourself, "What is a specific GOAL that I'm aiming to achieving?"

Then ask yourself, "What ACTIONS have I used that haven't worked or have perpetuated problems?" You will likely gain a great deal of insights from this question.

Follow on with some healthy, unedited, crazy, wild, outlandish brainstorming by asking, "What logical, crazy, insane ideas do I have which could be sequential steps or STRATEGIES to achieve my goal?

The final step, MEASURE is key. As I mentioned in an earlier chapter. If you can't measure progress, then how do you know if you're really progressing?

Peter Drucker had a saying which makes this final point well, "You can't improve what you don't measure."

TIME SAVERS AND TIMELY QUESTIONS

1. Imagine being so entrained that you couldn't stop yourself. You could do that with your time and focus. Anyone can do it. Just start a habit.
2. Feel free to use my GASM system. Start by asking, "What is a specific GOAL that I'm aiming to achieve?"
3. Then ask yourself, "What ACTIONS have I used that haven't worked or have perpetuated problems? And what actions could I take instead?"
4. Follow on with some healthy, unedited, crazy, wild, outlandish brainstorming by asking, "What logical, crazy, insane ideas do I have which could be sequential steps or STRATEGIES to achieve my goal?
5. The final step is to define specific MEASURES that you can put in place to determine if you are progressing well or not.

13. Mind Games We Play With Time

Playing 'mind games' with another person can be a pernicious undertaking. Though we can escalate that to a whole new level.

Playing mind games with yourself, well that's something more disorientating and limiting than ever.

It reminds me of John Lennon's song Mind Games. Lennon's inspiration came from a book he read called *Mind Games: The Guide to Inner Space*[1]. Written by Robert Masters and Jean Houston. It takes the positive route and explains how we can improve ourselves on various levels by playing tricks on our

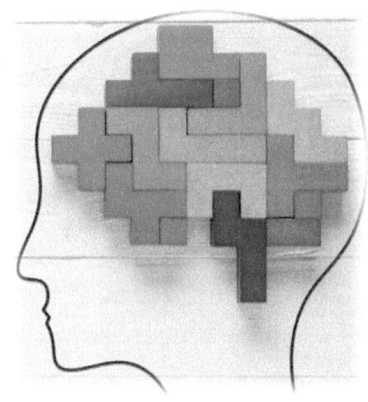

minds. The song is really about making yourself a better person.

Mind Games was the only single released from Lennon's Mind Games album. It was a modest success but nowhere near as popular as his Beatles output.

In a 1998 interview with *Uncut*, Yoko Ono posited that the song may have been ahead of its time. "I think that people didn't quite get the message because this was again before its time," she said. "Now, people would understand it. I don't think in those days people knew that they were playing mind games anyway."

While Yoko Ono is a clever lady, I would go one step further. From all the work I do untraining people's brains, I strongly believe that most people, still today, are unaware that they're playing mind games with themselves. That is until it's pointed out to them. I would go as far as say that any difficulty we are having in our life is due to some mind game we're playing with ourselves.

For me personally, before learning Neuro Linguistic Programming I realised I was playing many mind games with myself. These negatively affected my relationships, my income, my self-esteem and my overall happiness.

I told myself stories that limited my income. "I have poor parents, so of course I will struggle with money" was one such story. "Because I'm not as smart as other people, I'll have to work harder to keep my job." These are the stories or mind games that led me to accept large roles with small financial remuneration. Company recruiters took advantage of the mind games that led to my low self-esteem. I thank my lucky stars that I found NLP and discovered my limitations.

I once believed that as humanity got smarter that we would no longer play the mind games that limited us. Instead,

I see the intelligence shifting to the upper echelons of control.

Before I begin. Please don't believe that I only value high intelligence and good strategy. Because while I do value these, I also value ethics and kindness. Without these last two traits, cleverness can be cancerous to our civilisation. Particularly as people use intelligence against one another, rather than to support the whole.

The game that is being played all around the world is the game of distraction and manipulation. There are many individuals and organisations that want more of your time and attention.

Clever and strategic business owners have manipulated what we receive on social media through sneaky algorithms. Love him or loathe him, we saw former American President Donald Trump being aided by clever and underhanded social media tactics.

The social media giants convinced billions of us to put all our private data online and now charge people to use our data against us. You might not see it that way, though I promise you, you eventually will.

By the way, this is nothing new. Mind games and manipulations are rife through our history. Back in 1900, billionaire J.D. Rockefeller used his wealth to pay off scientists to provide false scientific evidence to sell fluoride to governments and dentists, and then to unfortunate populations around the world. Don't believe me? Fair enough but do your own research and eventually you will discover the evidence as to how fluoride came to be in our water.

We know too that fluoride is included in toothpaste, tea, coffee, artificial sweeteners, sodas, flavoured popsicles, baby foods, broths, stews, and hot cereals made with tap water. If fluoride fortified water is used to make these foods and drinks, they will contain even more fluoride.

Fluoride was a waste product, used as a mind control agent by the Nazis and promoted as good for teeth by companies that needed to dispose of this waste product and were allies with the Nazi's. Fluoride is a poison, but we've been fooled into believing it's good for us by clever mind gamers[2]. Of course, the mind games of clever manipulators of mind and money doesn't stop there.

Over 2 billion people play video games worldwide, and the market for video games was estimated to be a $90 billion industry in America alone in 2020.

According to *TechRepublic*, the average gamer spends 8 hours and 27 minutes each week[3].

But while we look at wasted time over a week, it's a scant view and a limited perspective. The truth of these figures reveals that the average gamer gives away 18.3 days of their year or 439.4 hours. Over ten years, that number rises to a mindboggling 183 days or 4,394 hours. Don't think that's a long time? Let's look at this another way.

If you're a regular gamer and you directed that time to a part time job or increased your work hours, you would now be enjoying a bounty in your cash assets. For example, at the average hourly rate of income in Australia of $34.96, you would have generated an extra pre-tax income of $153,614.00.

Now, before you start saying, that's not me R!k! I don't play games, or I don't play games that much. Think of the time you might be spending on social media or playing

Solitaire, Subway Surfers, Raid, Mech Arena or Mafia City or your favourite distraction?

If you play video games, you can be excused for the hold that they have over you.

Over 2 billion people play video games worldwide. The market for video games was estimated to be a $90 billion industry in America alone in 2020.

For most players, playing video games is a fun pastime: a way to relax, connect with friends, and enjoy a challenge. Unfortunately, for some, a video game hobby is likely to escalate into an addictive disorder which takes over their lives.

Video games affect the brain in the same way as addictive drugs. They trigger the release of dopamine, a chemical which reinforces behaviour. For this reason, playing video games can be an addictive stimulus.

The desires for escapism and social acceptance may not be the only causes of video game addiction. Numerous studies have sought to establish the relationship between video game addiction and other mental health problems.

One 2016 study suggested that people who are depressed and cope with problems in an avoidant way are more likely to become addicted to video games. Another study from 2017 found a strong correlation between video game addiction and anxiety disorders. Although it's not clear whether the addiction causes the anxiety or if the anxiety contributes to the addiction.[4]

Video games are designed to be addictive. Not 'addictive' in the clinical sense of the word, but game designers are always looking for ways to make their games more interesting in order to increase the amount of time people spend playing them. This is particularly true for game developers whose business model relies on in-game purchases.

> **There are several 'hooks' that are built into games with the intent of making them 'addictive.'**

Games that hook players are intentional. These are just difficult enough to be challenging. While allowing players to achieve small accomplishments that compel them to keep playing. In that respect, the design of video games is similar to the design of gambling casinos. Casinos will allow players to have small 'wins' that keep them playing.

There are several 'hooks' built into games with the intent of making them 'addictive':

The High Score: Whether you've tried out the latest edition of *Grand Theft Auto* or haven't played a video game since *PacMan*, the high score or completion percentage is one of the most easily recognisable hooks. Trying to beat the high score (even if the player is trying to beat their own score) can keep a player engrossed for hours.

Beating your Rival: More and more gamers are competing with or against friends and other players from across the world via the internet. There are many permutations of online competitive gaming. Some games involve forming clans to compete against other groups of players. While others use the last man standing 'battle royale' format, most famously *Fortnite*. Here the goal may be to rise up the leader board or to gain bragging rights over friends.

Beating the Game: This 'hook' isn't used in online role-playing games but is found in nearly every gaming system. The desire to beat the game is fed as a player 'levels up,' or finds the next hidden clue.

> **In 2017, I decided to do some personal research. I downloaded a game to see how addictive they were and see if I could be suckered into the game.**

Role-Playing: Role-playing games allow players to do more than just play. They get to create the characters in the game and embark on an adventure that's somewhat unique to that character. Consequently, there's an emotional attachment to the character, and the story makes it much harder to stop playing.

Discovery: The exploration or discovery tactic is most often used in role-playing games. One of the most popular online games of all time is *World of Warcraft*, and a good portion of the game is spent exploring imaginary worlds. This thrill of discovery (even of places that don't really exist) can be extremely compelling.

Relationships: Again, this is primarily an online 'hook.' Online role-playing games allow people to build relationships with other players. For some kids, this online community becomes the place where they're most accepted, which draws them back again and again.[5]

In 2017, I decided to do some personal research. I downloaded a game to see how addictive they were and see if I could be suckered into the game.

In mere days, I discovered that all my mindpower surmounted to nil. These game designers know the tricks to get you addicted fast.

The game I downloaded didn't even meet my interest or values! The game was *Sniper 3D*. *Sniper 3D* is an online 'Player versus Player' (PvP) gun shooting game. Here you join millions of users and start fighting in a multiplayer shooter arena. Your aim is to become the best sniper assassin in this multiplayer 'Frames Per Second' (FPS) gun shooting game.

I was not impressed with the game at first, as I had to ideally aim at the heads of other snipers and pull the trigger. Even though I was only killing animated people, it still made me wince. Surprisingly, in just days, I, the pacifist, was desensitised to killing as many people as possible in order to win or achieve points to upgrade my rifle.

Within a short period of time, I found myself getting quite good at the game but never quite good enough to lead the ranks or 'beat the game.' Until later.

As I improved, my 'high scores' gave me enough points to get a better clothing, armour, and weapons. The new weapons provided improvements to my aim and distance that were noticeable. This drove me to gain more points and within weeks of playing I was invited into a team. Yeeha! Someone out there likes me! Well, that's what it felt like but now I was committed to contributing to not just my accumulative points but that of the team's.

Here is where it got ugly.

My family knew that this was my research project, but they could see me changing before their eyes. I was showing all the signs of addiction. At every opportunity, I would be playing that stupid game. The research was to be for six months but soon turned into a year.

In your phone settings, there is a 'Digital Wellbeing & parental controls' function which tells you how much time you spend on apps. With little effort I could see that I was spending far more time than I would have guessed on *Sniper 3D*.

Most days, I would be playing that game for up to two hours and some days I would spend up to four hours! All this screen time while sitting with the family as we watched a movie. Any gap was filled; waiting on software to download, lying in bed before going to sleep, standing in a queue for my coffee order. It was insane!

This reduced my interactions with my family, and I dare say it also had me eating snacks without even thinking—as I played this endless, mind-numbing game.

I was fast becoming a major world player of this game, getting to number one in the world several times. I was winning the game but losing my family, and my mind! Finally, I had to end my research and delete the game. The question I had to ask myself was, "What did it cost?"

While the game itself cost nothing at all and I stoically avoided spending a cent on upgrades or daily advances that were offered to me. The game cost me a fortune.

I wasted a pre-tax income of $38,281.00 playing Sniper 3D.

Let's just call it 3 hours a day for 365 days that I played the game, even though I believe it was more than that. That's a total of 1095 hours in one year.

If we use the earlier example, at the average hourly rate of income in Australia of $34.96, I wasted a pre-tax income of $38,281.00 playing *Sniper 3D*. Though for privacy reasons, I won't share my real hourly income. So, the price I paid financially was much more. Though that wasn't the biggest price I paid. The biggest penalty was my relationship with my family needed some healing as I invested often, more time on my game than in them.

I know too that the respect I had with my daughters diminished. They would often say, "Is this still research dad?" To which I would say "Of course" with a smattering of guilt.

One day a friend came unannounced and interrupted me while I was going for the million in a timed tournament. I shouted, "Don't ask me anything now!" without raising my eyes from the screen. That's when I knew the game had to go.

It was so unlike me. I had morphed into an addicted moron. Though I forgive myself and you should too. But quitting is essential.

What you must understand here is that games, social media, television and all its game shows and dramas are all designed to trigger your dopamine levels. They want your time and focus and don't be fooled. They know exactly how to get it.

> **Few really appreciate smartphones and the social media platforms they support are turning us into bona fide addicts.**

"I feel tremendous guilt," admitted Chamath Palihapitiya, former Vice President of User Growth at *Facebook*, to an audience of *Stanford* students. He was responding to a question about his involvement in exploiting consumer behaviour.

"The short-term, dopamine-driven feedback loops that we have created are destroying how society works," he explained. In Palihapitiya's talk, he highlighted something most of us know but few really appreciate. Smartphones and the social media platforms they support are turning us into bona fide addicts.

While it's easy to dismiss this claim as hyperbole, platforms like *Facebook*, *Snapchat*, and *Instagram* leverage the very same neural circuitry used by slot machines and cocaine to keep us using their products as much as possible. Taking a closer look at the underlying science may give you pause the next time you feel your pocket buzz.

If you've ever misplaced your phone, you may have experienced a mild state of panic until it's been found. About 73% of people claim to experience this unique flavour of anxiety, which makes sense when you consider that adults in the US spend an average of 2-4 hours per day tapping, typing, and swiping on their devices—that adds up to over 2,600 daily touches.

Most of us have become so intimately entwined with our digital lives that we sometimes feel our phones vibrating in our pockets when they aren't even there.

If we think smartphones, games, apps and social media are all controlling our lives think again. It's us, not them that needs help. We are the ones giving over our power to others. We have succumbed to our own mind games justifying our time-wasting efforts.

Though here is the greatest of all the mind games we play. People give it all sorts of names. Overwhelm, stress, worry, fear, procrastination, being stuck or trying to get over the mountains of mindset hurdles. It all comes down to one thing: FEAR!

I have come to discover from all my years of coaching, consulting and training, that most people's problems carry an invisible cost that they are completely unaware of the price.

That cost is time. Time wasted due to stress and fear. Time lost due to anxiety, frustration and depression. Time that can never be returned from missing opportunities due to fear and procrastination. I believe most people don't value their time enough to know that a loss of time and purpose can be the greatest cost of all to you.

All resistance to growth is fear and fear can only be found in our unconscious mind.

Recently, I was interviewed on a podcast entitled, 'Under the Knife.' The interviewer and my friend, Dr Arun Dhir is a well-respected Melbourne-based Gastrointestinal and Weight Loss Surgeon. Under the 'Knife' series features transformational conversations with world experts to dissect modern-day challenges that keep us from ultimate health and healing.[7]

I was asked, "What are three of my personal truths?" To which my first truth is GROWTH. I said, "I believed that anyone can be, do or have anything as long as they are willing to grow."

It's true. You can be, do and have anything, as long as you are willing to grow. But HOW does one grow? It's not what you might think. I'm sure right now you'll be running a litany of books, teachers, courses, events through your mind, that challenge us, and grow us. You could be excused for thinking these things cause you to grow—but they're not. They are the vehicles to grow, but we have forgotten about one HUGE barrier to growth and that is YOU and your desire to remain the same, unchanged.

The only way we can truly grow is when we are willing to remove the neurological blocks that stop us from stopping ourselves. Oh, I'm sure that you can find many intellectual reasons for a failure to grow and they will all sound interesting and intellectual. Though I'm telling you here and now—all resistance to growth is fear and fear can only be found in our unconscious mind. No book or course can remove your fear. Not even my book "ROAR! Courage—though mind you, at least I have some tools in that book. Only *you* can remove fear by doing the inner work.

Something that can further stilt our growth and hinder our time is our mood. Dr. Arun Dhir had this to say.

"It might come as a surprise to you if I were to mention that the food that you consume has got the potential to influence your mood. Your mood is nothing but a collection of emotions, feelings and thought patterns that determine your attitude. The secret to understanding the link between depression and lack of focus on one side and mental clarity along with discipline of thought on the other could be found in an individual's diet.

"Another fascinating area of research is in the space of ADHD in childhood and its association with diet. The attention span of an average individual has dropped from 36 seconds in 1980s to almost 4 seconds in the current decade. Treating this condition with medications, without examining the diet would be missing the point by a mile.

"As a gut health expert I have been researching the subject of how our food affects our mood. There have been several scientific studies that have looked into this very topic however this one study published in *Brain, Behaviour and Immunity* in 2014 presented some very compelling evidence. In summary what they found was a strong association between depression and a diet rich in sugar, sweetened soft drinks, refined flour and red meat. Undoubtedly the food that you eat has a significant impact on how your brain functions. Clean, green and predominantly plant based whole foods have proven in several studies to have a significant positive effect on our mood and ability to think clearly."[7]

People have a natural tendency to avoid growth and change.

Call it a 'natural tendency' or 'self-sabotage,' but we all have a glass ceiling that we are scared to break through. At some level, all of us are fearful of growing.

People have a natural tendency to avoid growth and change.

According to Rosabeth Moss Kanter, the Ernest L. Arbuckle Professor of Business Administration at *Harvard Business School* and former chief editor of *Harvard Business Review*, "Resistance to change manifests itself in many ways, from foot-dragging and inertia to petty sabotage to outright rebellions. The best tool for leaders of change is to understand the predictable, universal sources of resistance in each situation and then strategise around them.

Here are the ten that Rosabeth found to be the most common."

Loss of control. Change interferes with autonomy and can make people feel that they've lost control over their territory. It's not just political, as in who has the power. Our sense of self-determination is often the first things to go when faced with a potential change coming from someone else.

Excess uncertainty. If change feels like walking off a cliff blindfolded, then people will reject it. People will often prefer to remain mired in misery than to head toward an unknown. As the saying goes, 'Better the devil you know than the devil you don't know.'

Surprise, surprise! Decisions imposed on people suddenly, with no time to get used to the idea or prepare for the consequences, are generally resisted. It's always easier to say 'No' than to say 'Yes.'

Everything seems different. Change is meant to bring something different, but how different? We are creatures of habit. Routines become automatic, but change jolts us into consciousness, sometimes in uncomfortable ways. Too many differences can be distracting or confusing.

Loss of face. By definition, change is a departure from the past. Those people associated with the last version—the one that didn't work, or the one that's being superseded—are likely to be defensive about it. When change involves a big shift of strategic direction, the people responsible for the previous direction dread the perception that they must have been wrong.

Concerns about competence. Can I do it? Change is resisted when it makes people feel stupid. They might express scepticism about whether the new software version will work or whether proposed changes are really an improvement, but down deep they are worried that their skills will be obsolete.

More work. Here is a universal challenge. Change is indeed more work. Those closest to the change in terms of designing and testing it are often overloaded, in part because of the inevitable unanticipated glitches in the middle of change, per 'Kanter's Law' that 'everything can look like a failure in the middle.'

Ripple effects. Like tossing a pebble into a pond, change creates ripples, reaching distant spots in ever-widening circles. The ripples disrupt other departments, important customers, people well outside the venture or neighbourhood, and they start to push back, rebelling against changes they had nothing to do with that interfere with their own activities.

Past resentments. The ghosts of the past are always lying-in wait to haunt us. As long as everything is steady state, they remain out of sight. But the minute you need cooperation for something new or different, the ghosts spring into action. Old wounds reopen, historic resentments are remembered—sometimes going back many generations.

Sometimes the threat is real. Now we get to true pain and politics. Change is resisted because it can hurt. When new technologies displace old ones, jobs can be lost; prices can be cut; investments can be wiped out. The best thing leaders can do when the changes they seek pose significant threat is to be honest, transparent, fast, and fair. For example, one big layoff with strong transition assistance is better than successive waves of cuts.[9]

The only way you can truly grow is when you are willing to remove the neurological blocks that stop you from stopping yourself.

The games we play in our mind protect us from ever truly knowing how scared we all are—me included. I too have coaches and mentors that help me to recognise my blocks and fears. They are there to help me remove my fears, to do the inner work, to improve my outer world and outcomes.

If you're courageous enough to remove those limits, then I'm here for you and what's more. I'll reward you for reading all the way up to here by giving you 45 minutes of my professional time to help you to identify the blocks that are stopping you. You can use this link: https://lifebeyondlimits.com.au/solutions/ But remember, it's just for you as a reward. Please don't go sharing this free opportunity willynilly with just anybody. You earned this[10].

TIME SAVERS AND TIMELY QUESTIONS

1. Go to your phone settings to find your 'digital wellbeing & parental controls' to discover how much time you are spending on games or social media.
2. Remove as much mind-numbing fluoride from your life as possible.
3. Consider what 'mind games' keep you stuck.
4. I'll reward you for reading all the way up to here by giving you 45 minutes of my professional time to help you to identify the blocks that are stopping you. You can use this link: https://lifebeyondlimits.com.au/solutions/

14. Use Your Triple 8 Time

A daughter asked her mother, "What should I do with my life?"

Her mother responded, "It all depends upon one question that you must ask first."

Puzzled, the daughter asked, "And that question?"

"Well…" her mother thoughtfully began, "Firstly, I would remove the word 'should' from your question because 'shoulds' will never lead you to a life you love. And that leads to a more important question. Do you want to live a life of value and service, and fulfilment or do you want to earn the

most money you can?"

The daughter's eyes darted from one side to the other searching for her answer. Finally, she said, "Both!"

With a faint smile, her mother said, "Then the answer will not be found in your head, but in your heart. Find the things in life you love most and decide to become an incredible master of them so much so, that you will bring joy or value to others."

While my mother and father were poor, they gave me this rich advice, "Do whatever you love." As a result, almost everything I did for a living, I loved. Sure, I took on a couple of factory jobs and laborious jobs as a teenager. They were just for the money and they bored me to tears. But everything else I loved, learned and became a master of. My only regret is that I just wish I'd learned NLP earlier and undid my mind games to play a richer game.

In our *Life Coach + NLP Practitioner* training we put up what we call our "$50,000 Challenge." It's where we show our students how they can generate $50,000 extra income annually by following our Triple 8 system.

My point that I hope you're getting here is that when we follow our hearts, clear our heads of the mind games that have become our illusions, we can now truly master our time. You have more time than you realise, and I want to mathematically prove that to you today.

In our *Life Coach + NLP Practitioner Training*, we have a mix of students. About 50 percent of them enrol to learn how to improve how they think and communicate. It's an excellent course to do just that but they also learn how to remove life-long issues. This usually flips some into the next group. The next group is around 50 percent too. These people want to start a coaching business and time is going to be a key asset in their journey forwards. How so?

Usually, when you want to shift gears and launch into a new career or build a side-hustle, it takes planning and time. So let me introduce you to your 'Triple 8' time system. Why do I say it's 'your' *Triple 8* system? We'll, you have it already, but your beliefs might be getting in your way (more about that in the next chapter).

While most people believe they only have eight hours a day to work or can only hold down one job, think again. It's not true. Let me explain this further, but I've got build a couple of foundations first. So, stay with me here.

In our *Life Coach + NLP Practitioner Training* we put up what we call our '$50,000 Challenge.' It's where we show our students how they can generate $50,000 extra income annually. We teach them to recognise their own *Triple 8* system. Here's how the *Triple 8* System works.

We all know we have 24 hours in a day, right? If we work for eight hours and sleep for eight hours, this leaves us with another eight hours to do whatever we like. It's time you can invest in rest or time you can invest so that you can enjoy the rest of your life.

So instead of resting you could be investing some of those eight hours in building your new side hustle. Some of those hours you may choose to study. Perhaps you might even decide to do some research? You may even choose to build a side-hustle that pays you over and above your current income. Without leaving your job.

We suggest to our coaches, to invest some time each week in building lead funnels to generate leads for their coaching business. Of course, we show them how to do that.

Then, we ask them to allow one hour each night to coach their clients—Monday to Friday. They get the entire weekend off!

We suggest they charge around $200 per coaching session (which by the way, this rate is at the low end in the coaching industry). This means that if you did that for five days a week for 50 weeks a year, you would earn a total of $50,000 in income. Not bad for five hours work a week wouldn't you say?

**It's not about managing your time.
Time will manage itself. It's about planning your time
and sticking to your commitments.**

Sure, at first, you'll be investing more time to build your funnels to get your clients. But it gets better day by day. Once you've established a great lead generating system, the time you invest in working on your business drops substantially. That's what we call it our '$50,000 Challenge' and it's all done using the *Triple 8* System.

Again, it's not about managing your time. Time will manage itself. It's about planning your time and sticking to your commitments.

By the way, if you are not familiar with our *Life Coach + NLP Practitioner* program or NLP, you can check it out here for free: https://lifebeyondlimits.com.au/free-nlp[1]

TIME SAVERS AND TIMELY QUESTIONS

1. Perhaps it might be valuable to answer this question: Do you want to live a life of value and service, and fulfilment or do you want to earn the most money you can?
2. What will you do with your extra 8 hours of your day? Build a side-hustle perhaps?
3. By the way, if you are not familiar with our *Life Coach + NLP Practitioner* program or NLP, you can check it out here for free: https://lifebeyondlimits.com.au/free-nlp

15. The Biggest Time Vampire Of All

Our emotions and how we feel make an enormous difference to how we perceive time.

To realise the value of one year, ask a student who has failed his final exam.

To realise the value of one month, ask the parent of a premature baby.

To realise the value of one week, ask the editor of a weekly newspaper.

To realise the value of one day, ask a daily wage labourer who has a large family to feed.

To realise the value of one hour, ask lovers who are waiting to meet.

To realise the value of one minute, ask a person who has missed the train, the bus, or a plane.

To realise the value of one second, ask a person who has survived an accident.

To realise the value of one millisecond, ask the person who has won a silver medal at the Olympics.

While time can change enormously due to our circumstances, I would like you to go deeper now.

One of the BIGGEST time wasters of all is due to something that most of us have enormous control over. Yet some of us have no control over this at all. I'm speaking about your emotions.

For example, have you ever found yourself working on a project or just beavering away at work and something hits you and you lose all your energy? Your drive and motivation take off without you? What caused this horrible inconvenience? One word: emotions.

All employers and business owners experience emotions. We all do. For most, emotions are akin to a rollercoaster ride. They're variable, contagious, sometimes hidden but influential states requiring constant management, and are a part of everyday working life.

Emotions affect workplace relationships and thoughts, attitudes and behaviour of employees and managers at work. There is an increasing interest by researchers and organisations in positive moods and emotions and how these impact on employees at work.

We become aware of our emotions when our work is disrupted, or our roles are changed. We can be overlooked for a promotion, or false accusations can be levelled at us. These are just some causes of emotions and you and I both know that these can trigger an emotional, downward spiral.

Workers' experiencing anger, sadness, guilt or blame at work can be distracting and result in lower performance. When our performance suffers this contributes to lower productivity in the business and overall, in your country's economy.

While it is sometimes hard to equate what a bad mood does to your work productivity, particularly when you're in the emotional state. Consider what happens to your productivity when you fall out of favour with your boss?

On researching this topic, it became clear that not much research has been done in the area of the costs of emotions. However, in the area of investments, much has been investigated.

As a coach whose clients include many investors and traders, negative emotions and limiting decisions are costly to this group.

According to investment risk adviser *Oxford Risk*, investors lose an average of 3 per cent a year in returns to emotionally driven investment decisions. A gap that widens significantly in times of steep volatility such as during the pandemic, research found.

During periods of high stress, investor losses can rise to about 6 or 7 percent a year from emotionally guided investment decisions. That number rises significantly if someone was fully invested in (say) equities were to have sold out at the bottom of a downturn.

Loss aversion is a risk for even the most experienced investor. Because investors feel deep discomfort selling chronically underperforming assets at a loss, many people in down markets will hold on to losing assets, and instead sell the things that are going up. Which is, of course, the wrong way round.

Conversely, some investors are likely to focus too much on the present, rather than the long-term picture, and feel compelled to take action to ameliorate short-term discomfort. 'Recency bias' is the assumption that because an investment is underperforming it will continue to underperform, or that when an asset is outperforming, it will continue to rise in value. This causes investors to sell underperforming assets when they are down, crystallising losses.

A compulsion to buy high and sell low costs investors 1.5 to 2 per cent a year, compared with buy and hold strategies, the researchers found. A desire to back products and services that feel familiar during times of uncertainty can lead to overexposure and under-investment or investing in things that are widely popular and likely to be overpriced.[1]

I'm not your typical coach, I have helped people get through depression, anxiety, post-traumatic stress disorders (PTSD), chronic fatigue and many other debilitating emotions. I know all too well how emotions cost us our time. Let me share some case histories to make this valid point. Of course, all names are changed to protect the identity of my clients.

John and his brother Mark are city born adults who decided to invest in a farm. Speaking with John who shared his story, said, "We had four years of water and five years of drought." The business folded and both brothers lost everything.

I learned this when John came to see me about the crippling depression, he endured for six years. He wallowed in his own self-pity for all of those six years. He took a job after the business's collapse and would come home from work and lay on the couch. He would obsess about the burden of his boss, who threatened his job daily if he didn't get his sale's quotas and fell to the memory of what he did to his brother. He only came to see me after his wife had a car accident and was furious to find out that her husband never opened the mail and so never paid the insurance renewal. My client had not only lost his house, and his brother's house, now he had lost the family car. The price of depression became evident and the price to fix the problem was paltry in comparison.

Time is your only true limited resource and clearing your thinking from emotional baggage or trauma is using your time wisely.

When you think about the price of debilitating emotions and what they do to erode time and money, this story while extreme, is certainly clarifying. Time is your only true limited resource and clearing your thinking from emotional baggage or trauma is using your time wisely.

Thankfully after coaching John, he is now back on track. He's productive and he's back earning a good income, and no longer suffers from depression.

Another client, Crystal, experienced domestic abuse from her husband who could not control his emotions. At the slightest stress, he would become furious and punch holes in their walls. I often hear people blame one another in these situations and pay the price of their emotions and the blame game that follows. Crystal and her husband separated and divided their assets—emotional cost number one—asset reduction.

They of course fought over the children and anything they could, just to get back at one another—emotional cost number two—unresolved anger. And three—traumatised children.

From the physical and verbal abuse, Crystal shut down. She couldn't function and so could no longer work—emotional cost number four—income loss.

Soon, Crystal was living in a caravan, traumatised and unable to socialise or function. Emotional cost number five—loss of self-esteem.

Crystal paid dearly for trauma and associated emotions. It took almost a year of coaching to resolve all the costs. Though I'm happy to report that Crystal is now fully functioning and now earning more than she has ever earned, and she and her children are living back in a family friendly house.

A study into television viewing found that the more TV we watch, the lower income we are likely to earn.

Whether we deny it or not, emotions are our biggest time vampires. When we are not functioning at our best, we even waste endless hours in front of another time vampire—the TV.

Did you know that your television viewing is an indicator of your wealth?

A study into television viewing found that the more TV we watch, the lower income we are likely to earn.

A study conducted by the *General Social Surveys of NORAC* at the *University of Chicago* found that 34.1 percent of American families making less than $9,000 per year averaged watching more than five hours of television per day.

Compare that with families making more than $150,000 per year, only 1.1 percent watched more than five hours a day.

Obviously, someone not working has more time to watch television, but the findings show a gradual decline in television viewing as incomes rise. Thus, working people making $30,000 watch more than twice as much television as those making $75,000.

People with the highest incomes have a greater drive to succeed. Television can dampen such drive, leaving viewers content to be entertained for long periods of time. To rise from an income of $30,000 to one of $60,000, you must want to better yourself. Television is more likely to instil a 'let them provide for me' or a 'blame everyone else' attitude than a 'I can do better' attitude.[2]

Now that we have a better idea of what our emotions cost us and more-so, how they can drain us of energy and our self-esteem. I implore you, should your emotions be hindering you or stalling your success? Do something about it. I'm a huge advocate of learning neuro linguistic programming to start to understand not just who you are, but why you think as you do.

TIME SAVERS AND TIMELY QUESTIONS

1. How much time are your emotions costing you?
2. Reduce your TV viewing. It may just impact your income.
3. If you would like to have a little peak into our NLP training program, here are some of the videos to give you some understanding: https://lifebeyondlimits.com.au/free-nlp

16. Twenty-Five Time Wasters

An older man, a scout leader sat among a group of young boy scouts around a fire one night. They talked at length about their day and then the mood shifted as one boy spoke up again about a problem with his boots and the blisters, they gave him. It was the same story he told anyone who would listen that day.

With that, the older and wiser scout leader broke the droll with a joke. At the end of the joke, all the boys erupted in laughter, filling the night with a refreshing lightness.

A few minutes later, the scout leader again proceeded to tell the same joke. A few of the boys smiled, but nobody laughed.

After a few more minutes he told the joke again. This time none of the boys laughed or smiled at all. To which he said, "You can't laugh at the same joke over and over again, so why do keep crying about the same old story about your boots and your blisters expecting a better response?"

You are either a person that gets beyond their problems or a person who is limited by them.

The wide-eyed scouts thought about what just happened. To which he finished, "Stop complaining about your issues or your life will be filled with misery. Worse, you will become a misery and people will stop listening to you. Start solving your problems instead, by taking new action otherwise nothing will change and you will waste not just your time, but everyone's. You are either a person that gets beyond their problems or a person who is limited by them."

Many years ago, I recognised that I procrastinated too much. Better still, I came to discover that I feared making the wrong decision and missing out. This came from making many decisions in my life where I did in fact miss out. Again, something else I learned from NLP.

Knowing how our problems perpetuate from our past decisions and the supporting emotional state. I decided that I would make decisions faster, regardless of how uncomfortable that would make me feel.

When I went to a restaurant or café with friends or clients, I would pore all over the menu reading every single thing on offer. Twice! And sometimes even thrice! So, I made a decision to look at it the menu just once and make quick decisions. Yes. It was bloody uncomfortable, but I did it anyway.

I even made more complex business decisions quickly. Now that was enormously uncomfortable. Though today, I have conditioned my brain to make faster decisions. I have built and conditioned my courage muscle.

As I mentioned earlier, Napoleon Hill once said,

"Successful people make decisions quickly (as soon as all the facts are available) and firmly. Unsuccessful people make decisions slowly, and they change them often." This cemented my motivation to be decisive.

Time is universal and as humans, we adhere to time every day. Every person gets 86,400 seconds or 24 hours every day[1]. Everyone is in charge of their time and what they do with those seconds. Whether you use them or waste them, there will always be either results or consequences.

Nobody controls your actions except you. Unless of course you adhere to the 'blame game.' If that's you, refer to my chapter on "Mind Games We Play With Time." No matter what the circumstances are, you can change them anytime you want if you are 'at cause' and believe in what you are doing.

Time goes by fast and the older you get; the faster time seems to go! How you choose to spend your time and avoiding time-wasting activities makes some huge and impactful differences in your life.

Though when we explore time wasters such as procrastination, we immediately see the time costs. Costs to our creativity, costs to the quality of our work and the financial costs. Though to start, it is important to know the meaning of procrastination.

Procrastination is the deliberate act of delaying, unnecessarily, what needs to be done. Some delays are necessary: waiting on permission, waiting on information, waiting on collaboration. But many delays are optional.

We choose to delay because we are avoiding something else. If you avoid work that you are able to begin, you are procrastinating. When you or others in your business procrastinate, the costs to your business start adding up[2].

Research shows that up to 64% of employees waste time daily on the internet.

Time-cost is one of the first things that comes to mind when we think about procrastination. When we procrastinate, we may be doing useful things, such as organising the files or returning phone calls. But useful things are not always important things.

Time spent on non-important (but useful) tasks is time we do not spend on the important projects. Maybe you did reach inbox zero. Perhaps you do have a really organised office. But how about those billable hours? Did you log any of those in by the end of the day? You know what makes money for your business: finished work and billable hours or selling those services or widgets. If you value your ascension up the career ladder, then what are the key performance indicators that are most valued by your company or boss?

Research shows that up to 64% of employees waste time daily on the Internet, using non-work-related sites.

Procrastination is nothing new, but the Internet has made it so easy—and so interesting to procrastinate anytime.

Let us turn our focus to the business owner for a moment. Let's estimate on the low end and assume that you—and your employees—only waste two hours a week surfing the web. You and I both know that the real number is likely higher but for the sake of this exercise, let's assume two hours. That's two hours a week per person. How many people are involved in your business? Let's again assume you have 10 staff. That's 20 hours a week down the drain. Could your business have profited from those 20 hours being used to help clients, finish projects, and bill more hours?

A study found that in the U.S. companies are losing $598 billion annually due to procrastination.

A study conducted by management consulting firm *Proudfoot Consulting* found that the time cost of unproductive workers added up to a loss of around 33 days per worker, per year.

The estimated monetary cost of lost productivity came in at $598 billion annually for U.S. companies alone. What is your piece of that very unpleasant pie? Statistically how many hours are you wasting each year and what is the cost of that wastage?

Divide your gross profit from last year by the number of days in your work year to get your daily profit average. Then think about the amount of time lost daily in your business due to unproductive habits. If there's an average time loss of two hours per day, that's 25% of an eight-hour workday. What could your daily profit average have reached if those lost two hours were spent productively?

Not all lost productivity is due to procrastination, of course. There's inefficiency, indecision, poor planning, and waiting on other people. It's probably not surprising to you that waiting on other people is often due to procrastination on their end.

Procrastination creates stress and costs creativity and quality of work.

Procrastination creates stress. When we procrastinate, we limit our options and increase the pressure. Job stress has a consistently negative effect on work quality.

Time diaries and work research shows again and again that creativity hides when it is under an immediate deadline.

When we have some room to breathe, however, we feel more relaxed and open. This gives our brains freedom to make creative connections and come up with unique solutions.

If you or your team members procrastinate habitually, you will face looming deadlines and high-pressure scrambles to finish projects on time. The result will be less creative work, and lower-quality work.

Job stress is a key cause of employee dissatisfaction, and one cause is procrastination.

Job stress is a key cause of employee dissatisfaction. If there is serial procrastination happening in your business, the stress on everyone is increasing in proportion to it.

When overloaded, employees tend to procrastinate more instead of less. They can feel taken advantage of, and they may also think that they are incapable of doing all that is asked of them. So, they give up. They doodle around. They surf the web. They procrastinate. And as a result, they get less done and their feeling of being stressed and overloaded grows. One question that managers should have in their tool kit is, "How are you going with your workload, and do you need any help?"

Even one person's procrastination can negatively affect an entire business. You can't eliminate procrastination entirely, but you must take it seriously. By refusing to let yourself procrastinate, and rewarding others who do the same, you set the tone for your entire business. That may save your business thousands, in hours, dollars, and, well, happiness.

Below are some time-wasting things that you need to stop doing. Let's start with procrastination:

1. Procrastinating: Making excuses, which in turn makes you dread the task you delay. Then it makes you feel guilty later on. It's time to break this repetitive cycle.

2. Whining: You will not get what you want if you're a whiner. Try asking for help or developing strategies to reduce issues. Then do something about it by taking some action.

3. Unnecessary Chat: Saying a quick "Hi" to someone during a random run or walk is ok, but don't stop to chat to anyone you don't know, and for no reason.

4. Gossiping: Gossiping is not nice. If you're doing it at work, you're being unproductive. If you're doing it in the school yard, then it can lead to a vicious cycle where people tear each other down rather than build each other up.

5. Pointless Long Waits: Trying to eat or socialise in a crowded restaurant and waiting for hours is boring. Think of the money you can save if you cook at home or how much more you'll enjoy the company without the stress of poor customer service and long waits.

6: Unproductive Longing At The Fridge: Spending time (5 minutes or more) in front of the fridge and staring at what's inside is fruitless. The contents will remain the same unless you make a choice. It's also a waste of energy and electricity. Make faster decisions and move on.

7. Doing Other People's Work: While there's no harm in helping others, make sure you do your work first and finish it before helping someone else. It will save you time, sanity and energy.

8. Worrying: Too much worrying when there's nothing to worry about is a waste of time. If your worry is life or death, then share it with a friend for support. If it's not, then find another way to deal with it. Go for a run or focus on a positive project that lifts your energy.

9. Hanging Out With Toxic People: Don't torture yourself by spending time with negative people. It will drain you and their attitude might rub off on you. Surround yourself with people who make you feel good and happy. Positive mindsets is where productivity gets its fuel.

10. Watching Commercials, Advertising and Infomercials: Has this ever happened to you? Turning the TV on while you have breakfast, and an informercial attracts your immediate attention, then before you know the sun is setting and it's time for bed again. If you want to lower your income, go ahead and increase your TV consumption (just in case you missed that in the last chapter).

11. Answer Your Phone When You're Doing Something Important: If you know that the call is not urgent, let the voicemail do its job.

12. Checking Your Email Every 5 Minutes: Yes, it's important to be responsive to emails, especially if its work related, but not every 5 minutes. Book some time out during your day to check emails rather than checking it randomly—or whenever you hear the 'ding'.

13. Having Micro Breaks Between Tasks: Sure, we all need a break, but some people believe they need more breaks than they really do. If you have work to do, then watching random YouTube videos in between tasks is a waste of time. You know you can get hooked watching and you may find yourself watching zit popping videos or earwax removal videos after 30 minutes.

14. Watching Bad Movies: This was something I was doing far too much. My neural program that wanted me to finish everything I started had me watching a bad movie all the way to the end. I needed coaching to change that program and thankfully it's now gone. It's a waste of time and money. Save your time and your sanity by stopping or leaving boring movies and move onto something else.

15. Antagonising Others: Don't be a bully. Ever. Even if you're stressed out, remember that the problem is with you and not others.

16. Running Errands in the Middle of Peak Hour: Sometimes there might be no other choice but avoid having to run errands at peak times. Plan ahead for a more orderly experience.

17. Pushing Your Views: This was a biggie for me. When I learned NLP, I had so many strategies that I learned which helped my life and I wanted to help everyone. Soon I discovered that not everyone wants to improve their life. So, I stopped. Trying to change someone's mind when you know they will not likely change their mind is pointless. Move on and focus on your similarities.

18. Waiting for Something to Happen: What are you waiting for? Go out and make something happen.

19. Having a Clutter Collection: Sifting through your clutter to find something that you need is very frustrating. To prevent this, you need to de-clutter in the first place. Put everything in order and then everything will be easier to find. Personally, I find that putting things back in the same spot will save you countless hours searching for car keys and the like.

20. Relationship Woes: Staying in a toxic relationship. Stop hurting yourself and be wise. Get out and love yourself or mend the relationship.

21: Social Media Dependence: Updating your social media status constantly. No one wants to know everything that you're doing. Really. They. Don't.

22. Watching Depressing Movies: If you're prone to taking on emotions after watching movies then stay away from depressing movies. Especially if you have stuff to do. For most people, watching movies should entertain you, what's the point if you'll get depressed after watching a movie? You might have a pattern that needs some brain untraining?

23. Explaining Your Chosen Lifestyle: They wouldn't understand anyway. Move on, live your life and be happy.

24. Solving the Same Problems Repetitively: The reality here is, that you're either not learning or you're not putting a solid solution in place. Take action.

25. Excessive Screen Time: This might be your phone, tablet, iPhone, Kindle, video games or TV. Have a think about how much you find yourself losing hours of time with your eyes glued to these screens.

Now I know that you might be serious about making some critical decisions about ceasing some of these time wasters. Though I'll share that the list is too large to change overnight. So, it will be best if you just focus on the first one on the list that takes away your time in week one. Then continue through the list until after many weeks, you have claimed back many hours. You can do it.

TIME SAVERS AND TIMELY QUESTIONS

1. How can you build and grow your courage muscle?
2. Are you spending time spent on non-important (but useful) tasks instead of on the important projects. But how about those billable hours? Did you log any of those in by the end of the day? You know what makes money for your business: finished work and billable hours or selling those services or widgets. If you're employed, it's all your boss really cares about.
3. Research shows that up to 64% of employees waste time daily on the Internet, using non-work-related sites. Keep distractions to a minimum. Besides, the IT department know exactly where you spend your time.
4. If you are a manager, ask your team every now and again, "How are you going with your workload, and do you need any help?"

17. Twenty Time Savers

When I first moved into the world of work, I quickly realised that school didn't give me near enough experience. No-one taught me socialisation in the workplace. I was completely ignorant of the hierarchy and how to address the various levels. My education sadly lacked any mindset elements.

This made me feel foolish and fed further into my low self-esteem. At school, getting something wrong simply delivers laughter or a lower score. In the workplace, getting it wrong can lead to complete expulsion and loss of income. It gets so much more serious in the workplace. Boy! I wish I had a coach back then.

My insecurities had me falling for

office pranks and I fumbled my way through tasks. Everything seemed to take longer than I thought, and my time wasn't my own. Though I quickly learned to be curious and watch and listen to learn.

I realised that the best way to learn was to implement as close as possible to receiving instructions. This happened by chance as I used to believe I was stupid and had a poor memory. Thanks to the school system of listen, learn and test. So, I would be told what to do and proceed immediately to do it before the instructions fell out of my head. Today, I know this as an NLP strategy called, 'modelling.'

Applying what I learned and taking immediate action, helped me to become a standout and I was soon promoted. Action is where it's at.

> **"The distance between your dreams and reality is called action" - Annon.**

I once heard a quote that said, "The distance between your dreams and reality is called action." Both you and I know that creating more time to build your dreams is going to be time well spent. Though the biggest excuse to non-dream execution is saying, "I don't have the time." That's why I've included in this book, not just time wasters to remove, but also time savers to implement.

Though it's going to require your attention and then action. Please put in place what you need most as soon as you can.

Getting productive is knowing what to remove and knowing what to include in your day-to-day rituals. Activities are great, but rituals are better.

In the previous chapter, we shared 25 things that waste your time. These are some opportunities edit your practices—delete if you will.

The next logical time saving question now is, "How can I save time?" Great question! In this chapter, I would like to share instead 20 things you can do right away to save time[1].

So, here are some tips to save time…

Twenty Ultimate Tips To Save Time

1. Schedule your work around your peak hours: This is one of the best tips to save time. We all have that time of the day when we know we are most productive. For some people, it can be right when they wake up. For others, right before going to bed. For others, it's somewhere in-between.

Regardless of the one with which you identify the most, you should try to schedule your work or most difficult tasks around that time. This way, you'll guarantee that your productivity levels are higher, allowing you to spend less time doing the same amount of work.

2. Get away from distractions: This is one of the best tips to save time that you can follow: get away from distractions.

An Instagram notification. A call from your mom. An email from that annoying salesperson who is trying to get you to upgrade your mobile plan. These small things can disturb your workflow and make you lose work time.

It takes about 30 minutes to refocus after you get distracted.

According to a study conducted by the *University of California*, it takes almost 30 minutes to refocus after you get distracted. These 30 minutes, multiplied by several distractions you get throughout the day, can culminate in several hours of time lost.

To avoid this situation, avoid all types of distractions you might have around you. Take your phone to another room and turn it to silent mode, don't turn on the TV, and disable all your computer notifications. This will help to save time and be more productive.

3. Digitise your life: We live in a digital world. The tendency is for it to become increasingly digital. So, why not take advantage of it?

If you are going to keep your phone close, there are several things you can do on your mobile phone or computer that will allow you to save precious time in your day.

For example, why not order groceries online instead of going grocery shopping? Instead of going to the bank, why not use the home banking app and avoid a long line?

All these choices can help you save time, allowing you to focus on more important tasks. Earlier I spoke about using an app to schedule your meetings such as *YouCanBookMe* or *Calendly*. These will save enormous scheduling time.

4. Schedule your breaks: Taking breaks is essential to keep productivity levels high. However, these moments are sometimes underrated. Because if you just keep working, you are not losing time, right? This might not be true.

According to some studies and surveys, breaks can help you prevent decision fatigue, restore motivation for long-term goals, boost productivity and improve creativity. All these benefits will certainly lead to time saved in a working day.

Which is the best technique to schedule breaks? About this topic, the opinions diverge. A study by the *University of Illinois* states that you should take a break once every hour. The *Pomodoro Technique* advises working for a 25-minute period, followed by a 3–5-minute break. An article by *Inc. Magazine* advises breaks every 60 to 90 minutes.

So, which one is the best technique? It all comes up to what works best for you. Try them out and discover it by yourself.

5. Prepare your day, week, or month in advance: One of the most important time-saving tips is to prepare things in advance. And it's obvious why.

By preparing your days, weeks, or months in advance, you're saving precious time in decision-making moments because the decisions were previously made.

Some of the things you can prepare and plan in advance are Meetings: prepare a meeting is one of the best tips to avoid leading wasteful meetings.

Here's a short list of some other things you can prepare in advance:

Work tasks for the day and the week.
Meals.
Workout days.
Your clothing choices.
Holiday itineraries, etc.

6. Learn to say "No": It might be hard to 'digest,' but saying "No" is one of the best ways to save time.

Saying "Yes" to everything might seem easy to maintain good social and work relationships. However, it can also lead to burnout syndrome and spending time on things you don't want to do. I know, I've been there too many times.

We can all agree that spending time on unnecessary things is time poorly spent. Your time is a valuable thing, and you should treat it with respect.

Of course, you can't say no in all circumstances, especially at work. But there are several moments when you can—and should! Try to understand what is important to you and what is worth your time.

When you have this figured out, it'll be easier to say no to less important tasks and save time on what really matters.

7. Delegate work: This tip is gold for all managers, project managers, or team leaders looking for an answer to how to save time! If you're having problems managing your workload and if you have the opportunity to delegate some tasks: just do it!

You need to trust your team and give them more responsibilities. Otherwise, what's the advantage of leading a team? You need to empower them. Otherwise, you're going to end up asking yourself, "Why am I so unproductive?"

8. Solve problems right away: One of the most effective time-saving techniques is to address problems as soon as you're faced with them. Waiting to solve a problem won't make it go away—on the contrary.

Delaying the resolution can have a snowball effect, where the problem gets bigger, taking even more time to solve.

So, when you are faced with an issue, try to solve it right away. It'll save you time and keep you less stressed out. This conforms to my earlier motto, 'touch it once.'

9. Track your time: You know how chaotic a day can get. 'Surprise' meetings and calls, more time than usual spent in traffic, and so on.

All these unforeseen events can make you lose track of the time you're spending on certain tasks. And how can you prevent that from happening? Through time tracking, of course.

When you organise your schedule around time, you're eliminating almost any chance of wasting time, increasing your productivity levels, and optimising your work.

There are two ways you can track your time: manually, through a watch or a notebook, or digitally, by using a time tracking app for example. Apps like https://timeular.com/ or check out some reviews here: https://bit.ly/3UaTDcP2.

Even though the manual technique is simple, it's not as effective as the digital ones. By using time tracking apps, you can identify gaps in your schedule, see how much time you're spending on each task, and use this information to make better use of your time in the future.

Tracking your time is one of the best ways to save your time because you're going to know where you're spending and wasting it.

10. Use helpful templates: Using templates can be a big-time saver. Imagine you have a big presentation coming up, where you must show the results of the last trimester.

You need to do a PowerPoint presentation, of course. What do you think will be the fastest: creating a presentation from scratch or using a template previously created which can be adapted to several occasions? I think you know the answer to this one.

Not only PowerPoint presentations but also emails, Word documents, and Excel files: these can all be time optimisers if you have the right template to use. At *Life Beyond*

Limits, we have templates for all regular correspondence; emails, letters, you name it, we've got it. When I'm coaching, I often hear myself saying to my clients, "Oh! I know. I've got a template for that! Would you like it?"

Spend a little bit of your time creating templates for your daily tasks and see the magic of timesaving happen.

11. Use time management techniques: Having the right knowledge in time management techniques will help you achieve more with less time spent. Some of the techniques you can use are:

Setting goals.

Dividing your work into smaller tasks.

Time blocking or time boxing (see: https://bit.ly/3DlDkTs).

12. Decide when you should multitask (and when you shouldn't do it): Multitasking can be a productivity enemy. When you try to focus on multiple important tasks at once, you might end up making bad decisions, overworking yourself, or even making serious mistakes.

This will all lead to extra time spent on those same tasks. However, multitasking is not always bad. You just need to choose the right tasks to pair up to avoid having too much to handle simultaneously.

For example, you can listen to a productivity podcast or any other type of podcast, while answering emails. Or even listen to an audiobook while you organise your computer.

These pairings won't compromise the quality of your work and will allow you to engage in two productive activities at the same time.

13. Limit the number of decisions you make: Making decisions takes time (and, let's be honest, energy). We need to make them every day, multiple times a day.

A simple way to save time is to just simply minimise the number of decisions we need to make.

Create routines, so you know what your next step will be at most times. Create go-to outfits in advance so you don't lose too much deciding what to wear every morning. Former U.S. President Barak Obama for example decided to wear black suits all the time, to save time.

Create lists when you go shopping, so you know what to buy and don't waste time wandering through the supermarket aimlessly. We have a shopping list on the fridge and every time we run out of something, we add it to the list.

These are simple techniques that can save several hours each day or week. Doing this saves time and energy to make quick decisions in the most important moments.

14. Reduce your social media consumption: Please understand that social media was created to be addictive. We all easily fall for that trap.

Imagine investing 520 hours of your year for zero results? Sadly, that's what most new coaches do.

Recently, I was working with one of my clients. I coach lots of life coaches. Her brief to me in the beginning of our coaching was to help her to get her first clients. She was educated as a coach. She had her completed her training and achieved her accreditation. But was still floundering in getting her first clients. I can't tell you how many coaches face this same problem. So, what do they do?

They do what they see every other coach trying to do and get busy posting on social media. No real strategy, just lots of posts. You know the sort. Positive sayings, insightful memes, the odd picture of their latest dessert conquest at their local café. All hoping to get noticed and get clients. Enter crickets.

Now here I am asking questions to find out what my new client's client acquisition strategies are. Only to discover that she's just posting every day and liking lots of people's posts. Then toiling with ideas of what to post next.

She continues to tell me that she spends about two hours a day, Monday to Friday posting on social media. To which I ask, "How long have you been doing that?" She responds, "Almost a year now." Of course, you know what my next question is going to be, don't you? That's right! "How many clients have you got from investing around 520 hours in the last year?" The answer shocked her more than me. "Zero."

By the way, if you're a life or business coach and you are too looking for ways to get clients, follow the proven, tried and tested strategies of coaches who are getting lots of clients. I highly recommend my book: *The Life Coach Millionaires* - https://lifebeyondlimits.com.au/product/life-coach-millionaires/[3].

Whether it be for the FOMO (Fear Of Missing Out), the desire to learn what our friends are up to, or just because we have nothing else to do. It's important to reduce social media activity.

Here are a few tips you can follow to achieve this:

Turn off your notifications: Seeing a notification creates a rush in our brains, where we just need to know who sent what and why. If you turn off your notifications, this rush is 'deactivated,' and the need to access social media decreases.

Put your phone in another room: Like the saying states—out of sight, out of mind. When you don't have visual contact with your phone, you end up almost forgetting about it. This will help you limit your time on social media.

Set rules and goals for yourself: This is a great technique to achieve bigger levels of productivity. You need to make a personal agreement with yourself, where you promise you won't access social media until you finish a certain task. Do this throughout the day and be surprised with how much you can get done!

15. Create a personal workspace: We can all agree that it's much easier to work in a space where we feel comfortable. And this becomes even more important when you work from home.

Creating a personal workspace will eliminate the time spent deciding where you should work and it can increase productivity and motivation levels. Besides that, you can have the chance to personalise it to your own personal taste—it's a win-win situation!

16. Hire someone to help you: Do you have tasks on your daily schedule that don't need your personal touch or input? If so, why not hire someone to perform them for you?

Hiring an assistant (or a virtual assistant) can give you time to focus on more important tasks or just relax (equally important). Given the chance to do it, I ask: why not?

17. Create a system to deal with your emails: Creating a process for sorting out your emails can save you precious time every day. Particularly as this is a daily task that most of us need to face. And how can you do this? There are a few ways:

Check your inbox only at specific times: check them every day, two or three times a day, at the same time.

Define a time limit for this task: 20-30 minutes, for example and use automated replies when you have the possibility to do it. As mentioned previously, use a template to answer your emails.

Always delete unnecessary emails: By implementing these techniques and creating a routine out of them (making fewer decisions, remember number 13?), you'll be saving time for more important tasks every day.

18. Work on your procrastinating habits: Statistics show that 15-20% of adults procrastinate regularly. This means that a fifth of adults regularly delay their important tasks and waste their free time doing basically… nothing.

As we previously mentioned, your time is precious, and you should always try to spend it in the best way possible. If you identify with this issue, here are a few tips you can use to stop procrastinating:

Make sure your workplace is free of distractions.

Make up a reward system for when you accomplish a specific task.

Bread down complex tasks into small steps.

Have breaks throughout your day.

19. Choose remote work when possible: Remote work became a reality for most of the world in 2020, and it has become a preferred working regime for many workers nowadays.

One of the biggest pros of remote work is the time saved on commuting. By working at home, you save time you would've spent in traffic and can allocate it to house chores, for example, or to just simply prepare your workday with more tranquillity.

There are reasons why some managers fear the remote working future, but, if your company allows you to work remotely, my advice is to do it!

20. Use my special technique (5x5 To Thrive):

Finally, I have another precious tip to save you time: Follow the steps in the next chapter to use a tool that I customised to increase my productivity. This tool helps to get me focused and highly productive[1].

TIME SAVERS AND TIMELY QUESTIONS

1. "The distance between your dreams and reality is called action." Both you and I know that creating more time to build your dreams is going to be time well spent.
2. Earlier I spoke about using an app to schedule your meetings such as *YouCanBookMe* or *Calendly*. These will save enormous scheduling time. If you haven't done it already, perhaps do it now?

18. *5x5 To Thrive* Gets You Productive

Let's get you prepared for your own *5x5 To Thrive*. Mine is a blend of the genius of Charles Michael Schwab and Warren Buffet's 25-5 Rule. But the key is in the two lots of five minutes that you dedicate to the task each day.

Schwab was the president of the *Bethlehem Steel Corporation*. The largest shipbuilder and the second-largest steel producer in America at the time.

The famous inventor Thomas Edison once referred to Schwab as the 'master hustler.' He was constantly seeking an edge over the competition.

One day in 1918, in his quest to increase the efficiency of his team and discover better ways to get things done, Schwab arranged a meeting with a highly respected productivity consultant named Ivy Lee.

Lee was a successful businessman in his own right. He is widely known as a pioneer in the field of public relations. As the story goes, Schwab brought Lee into his office and said, "Show me a way to get more things done."

"Give me 15 minutes with each of your executives," Lee replied.

"How much will it cost me," Schwab asked.

"Nothing," Lee said. "Unless it works. After three months, you can send me a check for whatever you feel it's worth to you."

During his 15 minutes with each executive, Lee explained his simple method for achieving peak productivity:

1. At the end of each workday, write down the six most important things you need to accomplish tomorrow. Do not write down more than six tasks.

2. Prioritise those six tasks in order of their true importance.

3. When you arrive tomorrow, concentrate only on the first task. Work until the first task is finished, before moving on to the second task.

4. Approach the rest of your list in the same fashion. At the end of the day, move any unfinished items to a new list of six tasks for the following day.

5. Repeat this process every working day.

The strategy sounded simple, but Schwab and his executive team at *Bethlehem Steel* gave it a try. After three months, Schwab was so delighted with the progress his company had made. So, he called Lee into his office and wrote him a check for $25,000.

A $25,000 check written in 1918 is the equivalent of a $400,000 check in 2015.

The Ivy Lee Method of prioritising your to-do list seems stupidly simple. How could something this simple be worth so much?

What makes it so effective?

I don't believe there is anything magical about Lee's number of six important tasks per day. It could just as easily be five tasks per day. Like my own *5x5 To Thrive*. However, I do think there is something magical about imposing limits upon yourself.

I find that the single best thing to do when you have too many ideas (or when you're overwhelmed by everything you need to get done) is to prune your ideas. Trim away everything that isn't absolutely necessary. Constraints can make you better.

Lee's method is similar to Warren Buffet's *25-5 Rule*, which requires you to focus on just 5 critical tasks and ignore everything else. Basically, if you commit to nothing, you'll be distracted by everything.[1]

Before I give you my *5x5 To Thrive* formula, remember what you've learned about value. To honour this new tool, it is helpful to commit to valuing your time. By the way, if you're not totally with me on this, let me give you a reason you want to say a BIG YES! to valuing your time. People who do, usually earn ten-times more than people who don't. If you don't believe me, try to get even a minute from a high net worth individual. Try to get the time of one of the executives of the company you work for—that is unless you too are an executive and a valuable asset of the company. Try get the time of a billionaire and see how far you go?

So, here's my tool that you might find helps you to master your time, I call it my *5x5 To Thrive*. It's quite a simple concept and one that has helped me to be highly productive.

How to use my 5x5 To Thrive?

Every Monday to Friday, five days of every week. At the end of each day, whether I'm working or not, I invest 5 minutes listing all the things I could do tomorrow — just in bullet points. I have 3 columns; *Must Do*; *Interested in Doing*; and *What's Bothering Me*. The classifications help me to get focused mostly on the important work which usually falls into the *Must Do* category. However, the *What's Bothering Me* category can often help to take stress off your shoulders. *Interested in Doing* is usually where I put my ideas. I find that they often get transferred from one list to another, until I have more time to focus on them.

Oh! By the way, I don't print out my *5x5 To Thrive* lists. I have a word file attached to every day in my digital diary. That way I don't waste any more resources than we have to.

I'll be sure to give you an example of one of my *5x5 To Thrive* lists at the end of this chapter.

Then, over breakfast the next day, I read through my list and prioritise my list from #1 onwards. After breakfast I start on #1, then move on to #2 and so forth.

At the end of each day, I start the cycle again. I invest 5 minutes listing all the things I could do tomorrow and I rollover the tasks I didn't do today. It's amazing how much you can get through and more importantly, it helps you to remove overwhelm. Its just a small list of five things afterall.

Overwhelm is simply not listing tasks or doing the things you know you need to do until there is so much to do that you can't even remember what needs to be done. Overwhelm leads to psychological shutdowns and ultimately depressed or repressed states and that's not good for anyone.

Time is the only resource that must be spent and can only be spent at 60 minutes per hour. We truly cannot manage time. We can only manage ourselves in time.

Feel free to use my *5x5 To Thrive* system and you will become the master of your 1,440 minutes each day. Then you will:

Reduce stress.

Get more time to balance your life.

Improve your productivity, and

Help you to achieve goals and get what you really, really want from your life.

One final thing about improving the value of time, you might find this useful. While the average person may have 595,680 hours available to them, most people will be sleeping for 198,560 of them or for 8,273 days. If you got up just one hour earlier or went to bed one hour later each day, you would have another 24,820 hours available to you. It was never about time; was it? It's more about focus and commitment; isn't it?

We cannot manage time; we can only manage ourselves by planning our time.

So, what's really, really important to you? Make it happen in this lifetime by valuing this second and making a decision to start now!

I use hypnotic audio programs while I sleep to create my night-time University — you can download some here: https://lifebeyondlimits.com.au/healing-audios/

TIME SAVERS AND TIMELY QUESTIONS

1. Create a word file with your *5x5 To Thrive* and include three columns with these three categories:

Must Do; Interested in Doing; and *What's Bothering Me.*? If you don't know how to create a word file, email me and I'll send you mine ☺ rik.schnabel@lifebeyondlimits.com.au

2. I use hypnotic audio programs while I sleep to create my night-time University — you can download some here: https://lifebeyondlimits.com.au/healing-audios/

3. Finally, on the following page, I've added an example of tomorrow's 5x5 To Thrive for you. To give you an idea of how I use mine and what it looks like.

R!K SCHNABEL

Rik's 5x5 To Thrive

#	MUST DO?	INTERESTED IN DOING?	WHAT'S BOTHERING ME?
1	Prepare for tonight's Radio Show		
2	Complete final edit for my *5x5 To Thrive* Book for December release.		
3	Close off Masters Earlybird before midnight tonight.		
4			Start revising Speaker content and manual for new format and for new students. Starts: 1st March 2023.
5		Consider writing script for new video: "What is NLP, really?"	

19. Your *5x5 To Thrive* Perfect Practice

Rebecca Soni, three-time Olympic swimmer and gold medallist avoids decision fatigue at all costs.

When Rebecca is not earning gold for Team USA at the Olympics, she is an entrepreneur working from home. As many entrepreneurs discover, a lot of small decisions that must be made every day can lead to fatigue.

To avoid decision fatigue, that reduced ability to make decisions or make good decisions that wreaks havoc on our productivity, Rebecca plans out her day the night before. So, she has less decisions to make the next morning. It's Rebecca's own

version of my *5x5 To Thrive*.

> **While some believe practice makes perfect, it's not true. Only perfect practice makes perfect.**

Here is a *5x5 To Thrive* notepad. It's to help you into the habit of starting your productive practice. Now, here's something I have learned about progress. People can sometimes confuse thinking about doing things for activity. I call this 'Thinkivity.' It's thoughts that believe they are activity, when they're clearly not activity at all.

While some believe practice makes perfect, it's not true. Only perfect practice makes perfect.

Activity is what will have you achieve your goals and ritualising activity is what is behind every achiever the world has ever known. May you too be an achiever of great things. So how about you start your perfect practice with your own *5x5 To Thrive*?

TIME SAVERS AND TIMELY QUESTIONS

1. Don't get yourself caught up in 'Thinkivity.' Take action now and start your own *5x5 To Thrive*.
2. Just to get you into the habit. Use the following pages to make a start for your first five-day week.

5x5 TO THRIVE

MUST DO?	INTERESTED IN DOING?	WHAT'S BOTHERING ME?
1		
2		
3		
4		
5		

R!K SCHNABEL

MUST DO?	INTERESTED IN DOING?	WHAT'S BOTHERING ME?
1		
2		
3		
4		
5		

5x5 TO THRIVE

MUST DO?	INTERESTED IN DOING?	WHAT'S BOTHERING ME?
1		
2		
3		
4		
5		

MUST DO?	INTERESTED IN DOING?	WHAT'S BOTHERING ME?
1		
2		
3		
4		
5		

5x5 TO THRIVE

MUST DO?	INTERESTED IN DOING?	WHAT'S BOTHERING ME?
1		
2		
3		
4		
5		

R!K SCHNABEL

20. Time To Ask Better Questions

If you have now read the entire *5x5 To Thrive*. Congratulations and Awesome! Hopefully, you've applied many of the strategies that I've shared into your own life. You've even started your own *5x5 To Thrive* ritual. Very cool!

Yet after doing all of this, creating the time you need is still a challenge for you. Then you may not have focused your time at the best possible apex. In other words, you may not be asking yourself the most productive questions to get what you want.

Conversely, if by now your *5x5 To Thrive* has been hugely helpful, I would like to give you one more gift.

The gift of asking better

questions. This one insight has improved the quality of time in my life, in so many ways.

Questions are the mechanics we use in which we aim to get answers. If you are not getting the right answers; the most helpful answers, it may be because you're not asking the best questions.

Let me share a few examples as this can be a critical pathway to generating all the time you need to achieve success. Let's start with contextual questions; WHY, WHAT and HOW questions.

Shift from WHY questions to WHAT questions.

When you are negatively triggered by something that someone said, it is terribly natural that we often start by asking WHY. Why did they say that? Worse.

Why am I feeling or behaving this way?

While this question may lead you to the source, don't go expecting your feelings to get better as they are most likely to get worse. Why? Because WHY questions typically give you all the reasons, rationalisations and justifications.

The WHY question has our brain pointing us towards confirmation biases and surface answers to confirm our existing beliefs.

We then start to place judgment or blame on ourselves or others, ending in the reaffirmation of what we already thought we knew. We stay there, simmering, wallowing, dwelling with no clue on how to move forward in a healthy and productive way. Asking WHY can encourage negativity and even cause our brains to mislead us with our own answers.

Instead, it is useful to shift from asking WHY to asking WHAT.

'Why' questions focus on the past, but 'What' questions set the path for the future. With 'Why,' we look for excuses, but 'What' encourages breakthroughs. 'What' questions help us go deeper, triggering our curiosity, and helping us to discover relevant information. That's when the light bulbs start to go off. We find clarity and uncover the path to action. When that happens, we can focus our energy towards creating opportunities to move forward[1].

A great way to use a WHAT question when you are emotionally on a downward spiral is to ask, "WHAT do I want instead of *this* feeling?" Your answer may be the feeling's opposite. Such as if you're feeling remorseful for example, you might answer that question with, "I want to feel grateful again." Now you can ask your HOW question.

"How can I get out of this terrible time-wasting feeling and start feeling productive and happy again?" Now that's a more productive question to ask yourself. Isn't it?

High levels of productivity come from high level questions.

The quality of your life comes from the quality of your questions. So too, high levels of productivity come from high level questions. Don't ask yourself, "Why is this taking so long to finish?" Because you know that WHY questions will only support and deepen your understanding of what's already happening.

Instead, ask, "What could I do to speed up this process?" When you find an answer that is helpful, then ask, "How can I implement that now?

Most people's time challenges come from asking the wrong questions. So why do we sometimes ask unproductive or unhelpful questions? I feel it would be helpful to first ask a better question. Where do our questions come from? Answer? They come from our thoughts. In fact, that's what thoughts are, questions and answers. Internal questions that we ask ourselves and internal answers to those questions.

Thoughts are questions we ask ourselves. Questions that we cannot resist but answer. For most of our waking day, we are unconscious of what and how we are thinking. So being intentional can make a huge difference to the quality of our time.

In fact, the reason most people don't get what they want from life is due to the terrible thoughts they are having. Questions they're asking themselves and answers they're giving themselves.

Here is what I mean. If for example, you are feeling tired and you ask yourself, "Why am I feeling so tired?" You are only going to get answers that will reinforce the tiredness. As you now know, why questions so often lead to justifications. Such as, "Why is my business failing?" A better question might be, "How can I improve my profits?" or "Who can help me to improve my productivity?"

To help you with this, I would like to give you a detailed article I wrote for my life coach graduates recently. Because you could ask yourself these same questions to help you in your business or to improve your time in your career. In fact, these questions may help you in many ways. Here's the article:

Are you wondering why your coaching, your business or your life hasn't taken off?

It's okay, I too was confused. At first.

When I started my coaching business. I was asking myself over and over the wrong question.

"Why isn't my coaching business taking off?"

Sure, I had some clients, but too few to financially survive.

Then I realised, "Hey! I'm a coach! Ask a better question!"

And so, I did. What was my question? That's a great question!

Well, in truth it wasn't one question. It was four questions actually.

These questions are four vital questions that every life coach must ask. You of course don't have to be a life coach, because these questions can help anyone get clearer (But of course this article was for coaches, so just replace the word 'coach' or the phrase 'life coach' with your work title). For example (read the brackets).

If you're not a coach (add your job title), and you want to grow your business (career) big time, here are the four vital questions that every life coach must ask. If you don't answer these questions, then your coaching business (career) will feel like you're collecting aluminium cans from rubbish bins.

Here are the four vital questions that every Life Coach must ask or flounder or worse, fail.

Here are the four vital questions that every life coach must ask or flounder or worse, fail.

1: WHAT is the biggest problem you solve?

2: WHO needs that problem solved most or WHO will pay you the most to solve that problem?

3: WHY do YOU want to help them? And

4: HOW do you help them?

Here's what led me to answer those questions.

When I was learning NLP, I realised how many dumb beliefs I had that were limiting my success and so my income.

As I was nearing the end of my NLP training, I had a HUGE epiphany that multiplied my annual income over four times! This epiphany led me to earn more than the then Prime Minister John Howard! But you're not here about my epiphany. That's for another time. So, let's get back to my answers to those four vital questions that every life coach must ask.

Here are the questions and my answers to the four vital questions that every life coach must ask...

Just for complete disclosure, answering these questions wasn't easy. So, I got a coach to help me, and after our first session together. I got clear. That's when I answered those four questions, and this is what they looked like:

1. WHAT is the biggest problem you solve?

ANS: *I help people who have issues with money. They want more than they are getting now.*

2. WHO needs that problem solved most or WHO will pay the most to solve that problem?

ANS: *People who are unsatisfied about what they're earning now. At some level, they know they could do better, and they know that their thinking is stopping them or limiting their income.*

3. WHY do YOU want to help them?
ANS: *Because I know what that felt like for me. How much it hurt me, almost physically when I worried that I wasn't even going to survive. Somehow in my brain, I thought I was going to die—or at best, become homeless, destitute.*

4. HOW do YOU help them?
ANS: *I'll help them to get the best mindset and tools with our Life Coach + NLP Practitioner program[2].*

Frankly, I didn't answer these questions all too quickly. It took me one coaching session with my amazing coach and one whole day to answer those four vital questions that every life coach must ask.

I got coached that Friday and I had the weekend off. So, I decided that that Saturday, I would sit down and commit to answering those four questions.

Hell! I was committed.

After all, I had invested so much time and money to be a coach only to fail. No way!

I'd already quit my job and had no other income. It was boom or bust for me.

What happened next?

Change happens when you commit with all your heart. Most people think about change, thinking they're committed when they're really not.

The upshot? I didn't waste my entire weekend going around in circles.

Change happens when you commit with all your heart. Most people think about change, thinking they're committed when they're really not. *Thinkivity* is the word that springs to mind.

I realised that all that was needed from me was to STAMP! my foot on the ground and make a full-hearted decision. A declaration to the Universe that I was IN! I was committed to help and evolve my peeps.

I was committed to helping me, help the *Universe*. (By the way. Replace 'Universe' with whatever or whomever you believe in. I use the 'Universe' often, so as not to offend any religious or non-religious beliefs of my audience).

Things can change just like magic when you make a full-hearted decision.

So, I said to the Universe, out loud and in my head...

"I'm doing this, and I need your full, financial support. I'll build the program and do the marketing, and you find the people that need me most. Speak to their souls, not their human (because I know how scared the human can be. And how courageous the spirit is).

Speak to their souls so that they get that I will look after them. I've got their back. I will help them to evolve and help them to make more money. How?

I will teach them how to remove their fear of money. I'll educate them on excellent money practices. How to escalate their careers and build their businesses. I'll coach them. Heck! I'll even do some of the work for them if I have to!

Send them to me and I'll do rest."

Things can change just like magic when you make a full-hearted decision.

I then used my answers to communicate them on my website and in all my communications. I got clear and so it was easy for newcomers to see what I was up to and what I offered.

Like magic, my coaching world changed that next week. I got my first positive sign that something had shifted as more people enrolled in my coaching.

Then large numbers of people came to my premium program, my *Life Coach + NLP Practitioner* training.

Fast forward to today... I've made millions of dollars. I don't know if I have helped millions of people—but I've certainly trained thousands of people who have helped hundreds more.

This all happened after asking four of the most powerful questions that you can ask yourself as a coach, trainer or change agent or in your career.

The question is—when will you ask and answer those questions? Perhaps there are even better questions that you can ask?

And if you already have—welcome to the world's leaders. Leaders who lead by asking better questions and those committed ones who plan their time.

I welcome you as a change agent, whose job it is to wake people up.

Because my friends—the majority of the world's population are in one huge, big, out-of-control (through control) trance. They're adults, still running off programs that came from their parents and their childhood.

Finally, if you know you're here for a bigger reason and need some guidance or help?

Let me reward you for reading this far...

Let me reward you for reading right until the end.

I have now been a successful commercial coach for 20 years with over 38,000 hours of transformational work under my belt. No-one stays in business for 20 years without knowing a trick or two.

So here is my offer to you...

Regardless whether you are coach, trainer, leader, business owner or merely seeking a better life. I give you now one hour of my time to help get you clearer and get you on track. Here's the link for you: https://lifebeyondlimits.com.au/solutions/

Thank you for committing to make it almost all the way to the end of this book (there's just one final chapter) and I hope I've helped to make a difference in your life. You know how much that means to me and I hope I meet you one day.

TIME SAVERS AND TIMELY QUESTIONS

1. If you need any help or guidance, here is the link to a free solutions session. You can use this once as my gift to you: Here's the link for you: https://lifebeyondlimits.com.au/solutions/

21. Guard Your Time From Thieves

Before I begin this chapter, I want you to know that I hesitated to share this chapter. I wasn't sure if I wanted to share this side of myself with you. Every time I reveal my research in this area, it's either crickets or I am soon found by the paid, professional trolls.[1]

My human paced about my office wondering if I was making the right decision to include it. It was my moral compass. My compassionate soul and caring side that decided to leave this chapter in the book. It almost didn't make it and as you read, you will come to know why. I do hope I have made the right decision as people need to know the truth as there is so much

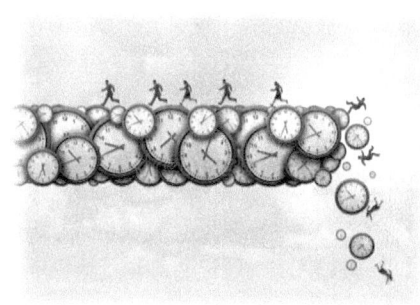

masking, manipulation and corporate malfeasance in our world today. So here it is. Unedited.

We've spoken at length about improving your relationship with time. Though there are invisible forces at play that steal your time. The final thing to do in order to be more productive with your time is to guard your time and your mind. Guard them from who or whom you might be asking? The truth is I don't know who these people are, not by name. But I know they exist.

As a crusader of consciousness and a provider of tools to evolve humanity, I have come to know that there are many people who don't want you to wake up. They benefit from us all being ruled by our unconscious programs.

**Humans are more profitable
when they are tired and distracted.**

Our thoughts, our patterns have been programmed for over a century now. The large majority have been brainwashed to believe myths that cause so many of the world's population to give over their money, their power and their time. Those I speak of benefit from humanity remaining uneducated and in a fog. Unconscious and tired. Humans are more profitable when they are unconscious, fatigued and distracted.

There are many who care not for your destiny and want to control your behaviour. Like offering poisoned sweets to children, these people know how easily we humans can be conditioned. Conditioned to buy. Conditioned to vote. Conditioned to rescind and give over our powers so willingly. They like to keep us fearful and then prey on our fears.

Our fears erode our time. Our fears make us vulnerable, and vulnerability makes us prey.

But fear not. I have only dedicated one chapter to this topic and in truth, 90 percent of book readers don't even get this far. Though the seekers of truth typically do. They go deeper. Much deeper than most will ever do. If I put this closer to the front, those people whom I speak of would have this book off the shelves before you could say, 'Salman Rushdie.'

These people are powerful beasts alright. I will never underestimate their reach, their influence nor their power.

These faceless people I speak of are beyond money. They have more than you or I will ever see in our lifetimes. It's not power they want either. They are beyond power. They have already taken the thrones of our future and have decided our fate.

There is only one thing we can do and that is to learn how to reclaim our consciousness. To stay awake. I'm not talking about staying awake while we could be sleeping. What I wish to be clear upon is to stay awake in our days and not to be in a daze.

Become conscious of your choices, so that you do not merely follow the entranced masses. Einstein was right when he said, "Common sense is a collection of prejudices acquired by the age eighteen." We must resist following the masses who by age 18 are mostly indoctrinated by people whom we know not their names. But we feel their influence and hear their PR campaigns through the mouths of our Prime Ministers and Presidents, and our leaders of business.

If you think our governments run our countries, you may be forgiven as by all appearances, it looks like they are the ones who make the big decisions. These people I speak of are beyond governments and beyond countries.

While I liked to believe that all people have good intent and are good in nature, that is not true. Not true by a long shot. There are people in this world that want to keep us dumb. Dumb and numb. Numb and fooled people don't use their time well at all. You might be asking right now, how do they do this?

There are many ways to keep people placid. I used to wonder why so-called intelligent people put mercury into our teeth. Mercury causes neurological and behavioural disorders. Symptoms include tremors, insomnia, memory loss, neuromuscular effects, headaches and cognitive and motor dysfunction. Mercury is found in dental amalgam, skin-lightening products, cosmetics and pharmaceuticals to name but a few.[2]

If you have seen the movie, Minamata you will also know that mercury is a by-product that is pumped into our oceans.

The *Chisso Corporation*, since 2012 reorganised *as Japan New Chisso*, is a Japanese chemical company. It is a key supplier of liquid crystal used for LCDs but is best known for its role in the 34-year-long pollution of the water supply in Minamata, Japan that led to thousands of deaths and victims of disease.[3]

Singer Robbie Williams almost died of mercury poisoning from eating fish all too regularly and was asked to stop or he would die.

You have heard my views of fluoride. That too in my opinion and from research confirms it too is a poison. Yet so called 'intelligent people' attest that fluoride is natural and small amounts will not harm us. Don't believe that for one second because it is not true.

Fluoride is added to 70% of America's drinking water, in what has long been a controversial practice of involuntary mass medication. As of 2016, around 92% of Australia's population is provided with fluoridated water through our drinking water supplies.

The CDC lists fluoridation as one of the top 10 most important public health measures of the 20th century. But a group of non-profit organisations is now fighting the EPA on this practice, citing a mountain of evidence that shows little benefit, and massive risks.

Not only has the ingestion of fluoride been linked to a variety of health concerns, but research increasingly shows that it doesn't even improve our teeth. Dozens of peer-reviewed studies show that swallowing fluoride has no health benefit whatsoever.

So why exactly do we fluoridate our water?

The origin of the practice is downright bizarre: In 1901, dentist Frederick McKay began a 30-year study of what was known as 'The Colorado Brown Stain.' Residents of Colorado Springs showed a unique disfiguration of their teeth: brown, mottled pits appeared in this population with alarming consistency. Yet, as McKay would soon discover, there was a beneficial trade-off for this unsightly condition: Those afflicted by the 'Brown Stain' showed a complete lack of tooth decay and cavities.

After an analysis of the local water supplies, McKay found an unusually high amount of fluoride, which he credited for both the lack of decay and the 'Brown Stain.' Today, the 'Brown Stain' is known as dental fluorosis, and mild cases (which only produce white streaks) are present in 58% of adolescents. This mild discoloration has been a known side effect of fluoridation since the beginning, but the benefit of cavity and decay reduction was thought to outweigh the risk (something science does with regularity).

In the last few decades, however, an abundance of medical research has emerged that shows much more profound potential dangers, leading to an ongoing legal battle to end this practice. Fluoride is essentially toxic to the human body, although in small doses, no acute effects are perceived. While our kidneys are able to filter out 50-60% of the fluoride we consume, the rest is stored in the body and has been observed to build up over time in certain areas.

One organ that is particularly susceptible to fluoride build-up is the pineal gland—the part of our brain responsible for regulating sleep and reproductive hormones. Sometimes known as 'the third eye,' this small gland has been linked to metaphysical abilities by many cultures throughout history. Philosopher and scientist René Descartes believed the pineal gland to be the 'principal seat of the soul.'

It is estimated that 40% of Americans have significant amounts of fluoride build-up in this gland by age 17. By old age, the pineal gland contains about the same amount of fluoride as a tooth. While the role of the pineal gland in facilitating psychic abilities and increased intuition is still up for debate, the fact that fluoride consumption impacts the gland's ability to function is absolutely proven.

There is no solid proof that drinking fluoride improves dental health.

And that's not the only part of the brain that suffers: over 30 independent studies have linked fluoride to a reduction in childhood IQ: A 2018 study published in Occupational & Environmental Medicine found that, for every increase of 1 milligram per litre of fluoride in a pregnant women's urine, their offspring averaged 2.4 points lower IQ scores at age 1-3 years old. This follows a 2017 study funded by the National Institutes of Health (NIH) showing in utero fluoride levels associated with lower IQ in 6–12-year-olds.

Animal studies have shown other neurological effects, including impaired memory, reduced ability to learn, and even mild forms of brain damage. With potential health risks like that, you would think that the evidence of fluoride's benefits must be pretty solid. Well, think again.

There is no solid proof that drinking fluoride improves dental health.

In a 1989 study, data collected by the *National Institute of Dental Research* found that children who live in areas where the water supplies are fluoridated have tooth decay rates nearly identical to those who live in non-fluoridated areas.[4]

You might be asking why do people knowingly put products like fluoride and mercury into our mouths and into the food chain? And if these substances cause us to have lower IQs and falling fertility rates? Then where are the benefits in these outcomes?

I used to think that these faceless people are poisoning us for want of money. I don't believe that is true anymore, because they have more than enough money. I'd prefer not to explore the why as it only leads to some very dark places indeed. My intent is not to spread darkness, but to shine a light to wake up those who fall so easily to become prey.

My younger sister, who worked for a pharmaceutical company that shall remain unnamed for legal reasons. She worked in one of their production rooms where they produced pills. She told me about the millions the company made every hour in just her department.

My sister was exposed to the powder in those pills every working day and while I cannot prove a correlation, she died of cancer well before her time.

While writing this final chapter may well have you declaring that I'm some conspiracy theorist. You may well be right. You may well be wrong. These are both your opinions and mine. Though the title 'conspiracy theorist' itself is designed to demean and discredit. I'm okay with that. One day the truth will set us all free. Though until then, I am not okay to feed my family accepted and endorsed poisons that include many heavy metals. But do your own research. Ask yourself, what do heavy metals do in the body and more-so, what happens when heavy metals get into our brain?

Your brain is a most precious instrument and is responsible for all you will do, and your productivity.

As a coach and an advocate for healthy brains, and reclaiming consciousness. The most common reason my clients give me for not being able to function at their peak is they cannot get their brain to do what they know they need or must do. Think about that. What causes brain fog? Fatigue?

Check out Anthony William's (Medical Medium) *YouTube* video entitled, "Mental Health & Toxic Heavy Metals."[5] Don't just take my word for it. Do your own research.

To master your life is to master your time, and the apex in which you must aim, is to master your mind.

Do all you can to reduce heavy metals entering into your brain.

My mission in life is wake up the world. I am not alone in this mission. I teach coaches. I teach trainers, authors, leaders who too wish to wake up the world. I hope you join us in sharing this book if it resonates with you. If this message mirrors your philosophy and if you too care about the health of humanity. Please share this book far and wide.

My final point is that to make best use of your time is to protect not only your time, but your mind. Your mind is the source of your future and it is mission critical to keep it healthy and free of poisons.

Closing Thoughts

I hope that writing this short book has allowed you to understand more about your time at a much deeper level. Weirdly, a book about time was the quickest book I've ever written! Words flowed out of my fingers in less than a month.

Our time is truly the only unlimited resource. Once you've spent it, it's gone forever. While some people squander time in the blink of an eye, others use it like a precious resource. I hope that after reading this, you fall into the latter category.

Time is so important in determining a quality life and so a valuable for crafting your future. Though sadly, few people ever invest anything like the time that you have invested in understanding time. So, for that reason you must congratulate yourself — you even got to the end of the book. Perhaps now could be time to share this book with the people you care for most or at least recommend it.

Thank you from the bottom of my heart for choosing to read this book. If you would like to drop me a line, I would certainly enjoy that. You can reach me via:

rik.schnabel@lifebeyondlimits.com.au. It might take me awhile to get to your email, but I assure you, I read and answer every one of my emails personally.

I know how much this knowledge changed my life and the lives of all those who I have taught. If you would like to join me and learn more about what is possible for you — visit our website via: www.LifeBeyondLimits.com.au and check out two great areas of the site, namely the "Free Gifts" tab and the "Training" and "Coaching" tabs — I promise we'll keep adding loads of resources for you there. You can also come and visit me if we're in the same city at the same time at one of our events or trainings. Please come up and say "hello."

If you would like to learn much more about how to take your career and your life to the next level? I've included a short snippet from our *Life Coach + NLP Practitioner* program in the following pages, it's an ideal starting point and hope to see you there sometime soon.

Warmest Wishes and Blessings

R!k Schnabel - Life Beyond Limits Pty Ltd

About The Author

R!K SCHNABEL is one of the most respected and knowledgeable authorities on behavioural change. In Australia. He's highly regarded as their #1 Brain Untrainer and believes that most of our solutions for attitudinal and psychological transformations will come from untraining our brain. He's an entertaining speaker that enchants audiences around the world.

R!k is also an internationally recognized and nationally accredited Master Trainer of Life Coaching, Neuro-Linguistic Programming (NLP), Public Speaking and Trainers Training and, an NLP Master Practitioner, Master Hypnotherapist and sought-after Life Coach and Mentor with over 38,000 hours of practice.

His previous books, *The Secrets of Creating a Life Beyond Limits* enthralled audiences with his profound insights into the metaphysical and the psychological world of wealth yet included simple principles that govern success. One reviewer exclaimed it is the *Reader's Digest* of Self-Development with its comprehensive approach to transformation.

7 Beliefs That Will Change Your Life is R!k's second book and *ROAR! Courage—From Fear To Fearless* is R!k's most necessary, third book and *Life Coach Millionaires* was written to help Life Coaches to learn how to follow R!k's proven path to coaching success.

Before working in the field of personal and professional development, R!k was a highly successful Marketing Manager for *News Limited* and a respected Creative Director in Advertising. He was also the founder of *Whozu Advertising & Marketing*, and *Schnabel & Knights Advertising* and an *XL Results Foundation* Member who helped to develop an Australian base for Entrepreneurs from all over the world.

When You Untrain Your Brain

After practicing the principles of this book, here is what happened to some of R!k Schnabel's clients and students of his programs...

At first my new beliefs expanded my paradigm of what is possible. Then they shifted my thinking and helped me to double my income! — **Vladamir Platil, Sales Executive, Melbourne, Australia.**

After experiencing a stroke, I was really struggling. R!k's training helped me to start believing in myself again and find my life's purpose — **Nikki Mennel, Entrepreneur, Austria.**

I now realize how my beliefs were creating immense blocks in my life

and I am having a ball smashing through those blocks, WOW! My world is continually transforming since my Level 1 and II Training with R!k and Life Beyond Limits. I am constantly sifting and finding gold nuggets throughout the whole journey. R!k's way of experiential teaching is absolutely priceless, a holistic learning experience which has impacted me to the core. — **Nina Shayan, Counsellor/Life Coach, Glen Waverley, Australia.**

R!k is an excellent trainer full of inspiration, expertise and always delivers beyond the promises he makes. His courses helped me to grow into a successful full time coach and trainer — **Mandy Siegel, , Coach and Trainer. NSW, Australia.**

I was asked to speak to 500 people at a finance forum for a major public organization about balancing their life and work. I did not believe I could do this. After one coaching session with R!k, I not only spoke with confidence, but my talk was so successful that people still mention it years later!!! This was my turning point and since then I have spoken in front of thousands and lives have been changed as a result. Thanks R!k for planting the seeds of belief so deeply that they have grown and flourished and many others have and will continue to benefit as a result. — **Dr Lynn Scoles, GP and Executive Coach, Melbourne, Australia.**

Engulfed by the dark clouds of debt and misery, spiraling down, captured and bound by the restraints of a limiting belief, blinding me to any possible way out, I attended one of R!k's training sessions and BANG! A light-bulb moment of realization and the magic of a belief change has given the sun permission to shine and the winds of change have blown those dark clouds away. Life is awesome!!! — **Rhonda E Abraham, Remedial Massage Therapist and NLP Practitioner, Cranbourne, Australia.**

R!k is brilliant at inspiring people to be their best by believing in themselves, as well as explaining the science behind beliefs for the sceptics. — **Pat Macwhirter, Veterinarian, Notting Hill, Australia.**

I found R!k's courses deep and insightful. Life Beyond Limits are always there for you. They want the best for their students and instil respect and dedication in all of us. If you want to excel in the field of NLP or Coaching, this is the right place. It's nice to be taught by a training school that genuinely cares — **Alf Garcia, Psychologist and NLP Trainer, Buena Vista Therapy, Victoria Australia.**

The best thing I did for myself was join R!k and the Life Beyond Limits program. R!k is an amazing trainer who delivers from the heart. His passion and integrity sets the course apart from all others. R!k creates a magical, powerful and empowering series of experiences that took me to a whole different level. The light bulb moments that triggered throughout opened my eyes to my unlimited potential. My only regret is that I didn't learn the power of Life Beyond Limits as a teen! — **Jenny Trad, NLP Trainer, Melbourne, Australia.**

Just do it!! If you want to know what to do with your life, find your passion or purpose, Life Beyond Limits will encourage these out of you. Absolutely fantastic! — **Luanne Marron, Director of Goddess on Purpose, Australia.**

R!k is all heart. He is a passionate writer, coach and change agent. His ability to see beyond what is evident is incredibly empowering. I now have a new career which I love and for the first time, my business is growing and I'm being financially rewarded, WOW! — **Jill Hosken General & Funeral Celebrant, Melbourne, Australia.**

R!k Schnabel is the most passionate and charismatic person I know whose very presence demands action! — **Heather Kaesler, Adelaide, South Australia.**

I listen to R!k's Hypnotic CDs three to four times a week — they're like magic every time. I relax, I learn and I usually discover something new about myself! — **Michelle Anthony Reiche, Business Owner, Hampton, Australia.**

Before doing R!k's courses I was stuck spinning my wheels trying to get into coaching. This got me past the fork in the road and helped me to flesh out my program. Now I'm easily producing content and it's now my turn to enjoy a whole new level of income, and freedom – **Matt Tait, Fork In Road Coaching, Queensland, Australia.**

R!k's courses blew my mind! They showed me how wrong my mindset was. I have turned a corner. The courses encouraged me to manifest and think positively. My first manifestations are coming to fruition. Friends and Family have noticed a huge shift in the way I speak and act. (Even on the telephone) For anybody who is looking at R!k's courses, don't think, get in. You will not regret it, I promise – **Andre Bothe, Geni(us) Coaching, South Australia.**

I was at a point where my life was in turmoil. I was depressed, anxious and I could barely get out of bed. In fact, the only way forward I could see was to end my life. My mum encouraged me to get coached by R!k and although I was sceptical, I booked in. My life changed completely from that point. Firstly, I'm alive! And no more depression or anxiety. Issues that plagued me for 20 years. I am no able to regulate my emotions which has had a positive effect on my personal and professional life. Best of all. With continued coaching, I have found my purpose in life and now help others like me to overcome similar issues. I highly recommend studying NLP with R!k – **Rebekah King, Director of Coaching, Moonbeam Monday, Adelaide, Australia.**

I had depression for six years, under psychiatric care and medicated for four of those years. In one session with R!k I overcame depression! I couldn't believe it was possible, now I do. — **Michael James, Sales Executive, Melbourne, Australia.**

I now know without a shadow of doubt that there is this great creative process that helps us to manifest; it's all here and now. Thanks a million, no, actually thanks two million! — **Steven Kolakowski, Melbourne, Australia.**

R!k helped me to more than double my income! I encouraged my whole family to do his Life Coach + NLP Practitioner program. It's life changing! — **Hector Ojea, , MD, CIMC Vehicle Australia. Melbourne, Australia.**

I'm the best I've been in 30 years and my family even say I look better, and it's all due to removing my blocks and my renewed motivation – **Andrew McGowan, Retail Sales, Victoria Australia.**

For 30 years I felt a deep sadness and loneliness from a family tragedy. In one session all that dross just melted away. You can truly be free with NLP tools and processes and R!k's coaching expertise – **Phil Hale, Teacher, NSW Australia.**

Other Books By The Author

A Richer Way To Think (Formally, The Secrets To Creating A Life Beyond Limits)

In this updated edition of this best-selling book, R!k Schnabel shows you how to harness and use the power of a Rich Mind, a unique system of thought-training and positive thinking that will enable you to live more successfully. Using a mix of personal experience, philosophy, and professional techniques, Schnabel shows you how settling for less from yourself is a choice, not destiny. Schnabel's teachings have touched people all over the world and are powerful but, best of all, easy. This book will show you how to develop

practical habits that will move you beyond your limitations.

ROAR! Courage — From Fear to Fearless.

Discover the real essence of courage and what most have missed. After ten years of research on overcoming fear and with over 38,000 coaching and training hours teaching the science of success, R!k Schnabel (Australia's #1 Brain Untrainer) shares his psychological breakthrough that will have you become more intimate with courage. We will soon realize how fear brings about fatigue, anxiety, stress and how it ages us. In the first four chapters, we quickly gain a practical and a psychological edge that will shift us from fear to fearless. Later in the book we discover the similarities between the addicted personality and the entrepreneur, and how we can use this formula to achieve anything we set our mind to. This alone makes fascinating reading. Vanquish fear and anxiety forever.

The Life Coach Millionaires

Get the complete client getting strategies from the millionaires of life coaching. Their secrets are found in the strategies they use. These elite coaches walk their talk and all have studied the best of the best in business and coaching. You are about to learn their strategies and understand their philosophies so you can duplicate them in your business.

R!k Schnabel is a leader in coaching, he's Australia's top Brain Untrainer and draws upon his thirteen years of research, and best coaching practices.

His background in advertising, marketing and sales, as well as his thirteen years as a highly paid life coach will help you to fast-track your business to coaching success. Learn the "absolute musts" and the "never do's" of life coaching. Discover the step-by-step tactics of the life coaching millionaires. You will learn how R!k Schnabel makes the average Australian's income in a weekend and lives a life of leisure and joy.

He lives an aspirational life near the ocean of Australia's New South Wales Sapphire Coast where he surfs with dolphins, plays music and writes. These days, most of his working life (if you can call it "work") is teaching life coaches how to coach and become successful.

7 Beliefs That Will Change Your Life

Our beliefs determine everything we can do and everything we cannot. The beliefs of our presidents, prime ministers, and leaders determine the state of our nations. Their beliefs hold enormous power, as do ours. Yet little time, if any, is invested in determining our beliefs or changing them. *7 Beliefs That Will Change Your Life* will give you the tools and the insights you need to move your career and your life forward. You will know your beliefs more intimately, and you will also discover how you can change them.

R!k Schnabel's books are available at your local bookstore (Australia, the United Kingdom, and New Zealand) or purchase them today via

https://lifebeyondlimits.com.au/life-beyond-limits-shop/ or via www.amazon.com.au .

Life Coach + NLP Practitioner Training

Imagine what your life, relationships and career would look like if nothing held you back?

At some level, do you feel or believe you could be more, do more and have more? Let us show you how with the latest advances in neurological transformational tools.

When you start our *Life Coach + NLP Training* you will learn to evolve and improve how you think. But that's not all. We'll teach you tools, techniques and systems to completely transform any area of your life. If you would like to take your life or career to the next level, then this course will likely become the

best course you have ever completed.

You might be saying, "But I don't want to become a Life Coach?" and that's perfectly okay. Only 50% of our students do. However, learning Life Coaching and NLP this way not only teaches you the tools that the world's best Life Coaches use, but you'll learn how to use those tools on yourself to create the biggest shifts in your life.

We learn how to drive a car. Why aren't taught to drive our minds?

You can learn this accredited course from anywhere in the world from your own computer!

Imagine if you could learn how to manage your emotional roller coaster? Create empowered states in an instant? What if you could remove all the limitations in your life? Particularly the limits that hold you back from creating more joy, energy, love and wealth in your life. Your picture of your future is about to get brighter and the weight you carry on your shoulders is going to get lighter. As you learn the most powerful NLP tools to creating the life of your dreams.

Life Beyond Limits Life Coach + NLP Practitioner course is nationally accredited and internationally recognised. This course provides you the tools to take back the control of your life. Learn how to evolve your beliefs. Discover how to manage your emotional states and gain much higher levels of confidence. As you build deep level rapport with those around you.

This *Life Coach + NLP Practitioner training* will be a course you will use for the rest of your life to create the best of your life!

What Others Thought About This Course?

"Just do it! If you want to know what to do with your life, find your passion or purpose, R!k will encourage these out of you in Masters. Absolutely Fantastic!" – **Luanne Simmons, Goddess Playshops Director, Victoria Australia**

"The experience is not only about changing, it is about tapping into your personal power." – **Denise Bonanni, Victoria Australia**

"Awesome! A course that will touch your heart so you can find your way." – **Michelle Rupuha, Queensland, Australia**

"Wow! What an empowering course! The 'AHA!' has arrived!" – **Steven Kolakowski, Australia Post, Victoria Australia**

Some of WHAT YOU WILL LEARN in the Life Coach + NLP Practitioner's Certificate Course:

Increase your Charisma by discovering the 4 styles of communication and improve your language skills so that everyone can not only understand you, but also improve relationships in an instant!

Be a Master of Success by learning the "5 Principles for Success" and how to create success patterns in your life and career that really work.

Learn how to Model Success Strategies as you discover the art of unpacking a strategy so that you can model any successful behaviour and install it into your neurology – this is often where the greatest successes are found in this course.

Dramatically Improve Relationships by mastering the art of rapport.

Improve your Memory and recall names and events in an instant.

Learn Easily and Effortlessly with one simple insight that will improve your ability to absorb information in a logical and powerful way.

Remove Limiting Beliefs that cause unconscious self-sabotage patterns in your life.

Remove Negative Emotions including sadness, anger, blame, guilt and fear that cause failure patterns in your career and relationships.

Shift your Emotional State in an instant with a powerful insight that you will use for the rest of your life just by snapping your fingers (no joke!).

Intercept Other People's Thought Patterns by understanding what their eye patterns really mean.

Remove any phobia or fear within minutes (yes that's literal!).

Learn the art of Hypnosis and why people are in trance 95% of the time.

Become a master communicator and why people speak like they do.

Discover your preferred Communication System and how to use it to become understood by others.

Learn the Art of Asking Better and More Powerful Questions to gain results for self and all.

Change Your Life Story to regain your control of life and your results.

Master the World's Most Powerful Coaching System to get results for self and others.

Learn Conversational and Deep Level Hypnosis so you can reprogram your unconscious to empower your success mindset.

Get Free Coaching for Life by tapping into Life Beyond Limits Coaching Network.

Design Your Destiny using all the NLP tools for success.

You can find out more here: https://lifebeyondlimits.com.au/life-coach-and-nlp-practitioner-training/

Bibliography

Chapter 1: Your Diary Time Saver

1. You Can Book Me. YouCanBookMe Pty Ltd. 38 Mill Street, Bedford, MK40 3HD, United Kingdom. Accessed 30 October 2022. Link: https://free-chat-with-rik.youcanbook.me/

Chapter 2: Time: Your Only Limited Resource

1. 7 True Stories Of People Building Incredibly Productive Morning Routines. Benjamin Spall. 17 May, 2018. Accessed 15 November 2018. Link: http://bit.ly/3O5PlBs.

Chapter 3: How Do You Measure Your Time?

1. The World's Broken Workplace. Jim Clifton. Gallup. 13 June 2017. Accessed 15 November 2022. Link: http://bit.ly/3O6MxUI.

2. Why Happy Employees Are 12% More Productive. Jonha Revesencio. FastCompany. 22 July 2015. Accessed 21 November 2022. Link: http://bit.ly/3UVowTb.

3. Speaker Training. Life Beyond Limits Pty Ltd. PO Box 722, Merimbula NSW Australia 2548. Accessed 31 October 2022. Link: https://bit.ly/3ffGQqJ

4. Trainer Training. Life Beyond Limits Pty Ltd. PO Box 722, Merimbula NSW Australia 2548. Accessed 31 October 2022. Link: https://bit.ly/3Ni1fId

Chapter 4: A Career Or Calling?

1. Your Most Passionate Employees May Not Be Your Top Performers. Winnie Jiang. Harvard Business Review. 22 October 2021. Accessed 14 November 2022. Link: http://bit.ly/3UX2EH6

Chapter 5: More Value Equals More Time

1. Cost of Smoking. Quit. Accessed 4 December 2022. Link: https://www.quit.org.au/tools/cost-smoking/
2. New Employee Study Shows Recognition Matters More Than Money. How you feel is more important than what you earn. Mind of the Manager. Victor Lipman. 13 June 2013. Accessed 31 October 2022. Link: https://bit.ly/3fmTFzs

Chapter 6: What's Your Power Time?

1. Money Magic Program. R!k Schnabel. Life Beyond Limits Pty Ltd. PO Box 722, Merimbula NSW Australia 2548. Accessed 31 October 2022. Link: https://bit.ly/3gWguui

2. A Richer Way To Think. R!k Schnabel. Life Beyond Limits Pty Ltd. PO Box 722, Merimbula NSW Australia 2548. Accessed 31 October 2022. Link: https://bit.ly/3TSxSyx

Chapter 9: Time Is An Illusion

1. 7 Beliefs That Will Change Your Life. R!k Schnabel. Life Beyond Limits Pty Ltd. PO Box 722, Merimbula NSW Australia 2548. Accessed 31 October 2022. Link: https://bit.ly/3UsBJm3

2. David Rock and Jeffrey Schwartz, The Neuroscience of Leadership, http://www.strategy-business.com/article/06207

3. Wikipedia 2011, List of Countries by Life Expectancy, http://en.wikipedia.org/wiki/List_of_countries_by_life_expectancy

4. David Rock and Jeffrey Schwartz, The Neuroscience of Leadership, http://www.strategy-business.com/article/06207

5x5 TO THRIVE

Chapter 10: Distraction Or Action?

1. How TV Influences Your Mind Through Hypnosis. Hanan Parvez. May 18, 2021 Accessed 4 November, 2022. Link: http://bit.ly/3DEiuz1

2. How Customers Think. Neuromarketing. Roger Dooley. Accessed 31 October 2022. Link: https://bit.ly/3U5lDOI
3. What Is Focus Time And How Does It Impact Productivity? GetClockwise. Alyssa Towns. 11 February 2020. Accessed 31 October 2022. Link: https://bit.ly/3Dqy29z
4. The Price of Distraction Is Far Beyond Your Imagination. Lifehack. Leon Ho. Accessed 4 November 2022. Link: http://bit.ly/3U7uvUu

Chapter 11: Systemise To Save Time

1. Master Coach + NLP Master Practitioner program with R!k Schnabel. Life Beyond Limits Pty Ltd. PO Box 722, Merimbula NSW Australia 2548. Accessed 10 November 2022. Link: https://lifebeyondlimits.com.au/master-coach-and-nlp-master-practitioner/ .

Chapter 12: Mind Games We Play With Time

1. Mind Games: The Guide To Inner Space. Robert Masters PhD. and Jean Houston PhD. Red Wheel/Weiser Publishing. Republished 25 December 1998. Accessed 19 November 2022. http://bit.ly/3hWNP8F

2. Draft NHMRC Information Paper: Effects Of Water Fluoridation On Dental And Other Health Outcomes. Christos Koupparis. National Health And Medical Research Council – Australian Government. 4 July 2017. Accessed 19 November 2022. http://bit.ly/3ggTxSu

3. 8 Hours and 27 Minutes. That's How Long The Average Gamer Plays Each Week. Tech Republic, Veronica Combs in Innovation, March 10, 2021, 6:04 PST. Link: https://tek.io/3zrLtox

4. Full Time Average Salary in Australia 2022, Talent.com Accessed 29 October 2022. Link: https://bit.ly/3gUlEqq

5. Understanding Video Game Addiction. Video Game Addiction. Accessed 4 November 2022. Link: http://bit.ly/3NGUwYA

6. What Makes A Video Game Addictive? Video Game Addiction Org. Accessed 4 November 2022. Link: http://bit.ly/3ftjPAN

7. Ten Reasons People Resist Change. Rosabeth Moss Kanter. Harvard Business Review. 25 September 2012. Accessed 7 November 2022. Link: http://bit.ly/3t4tq3X

8. Dr. Arun Dhir. Gut Health Expert. 17 December 2022.

9. Under The Knife with Dr. Arun Dhir. Accessed 7 November 2022. Link: http://bit.ly/3zRA4hL

10. A Solutions Session with R!k Schnabel. Life Beyond Limits Pty Ltd. PO Box 722, Merimbula NSW Australia 2548. Accessed 7 November 2022. Link: https://bit.ly/3E7nJJ2

Chapter 13: Use Your Triple 8 Time

1. Life Coach + NLP Practitioner program with R!k Schnabel. Life Beyond Limits Pty Ltd. PO Box 722, Merimbula NSW Australia 2548. Accessed 8 November 2022. Link: https://lifebeyondlimits.com.au/free-nlp.

Chapter 14: The Biggest Time Vampire Of All

1. Emotions Cost Investors Dear, Research Finds. Madison Darbyshire. Financial Times. 24 October 2020. Accessed 8 November 2022. Link: http://bit.ly/3UA7eKW .

2. Study: Poverty And High Rates of TV Viewing Are Linked. Movie Guide. Accessed 12 November 2022. Link: http://bit.ly/3WWRDXx .

Chapter 15: Twenty-Five Time Wasters

1. 25 Time Wasting Activities You're Doing Everyday. Get Organized Wizard, Jon Capistrano, February 25, 2018, Accessed 29 October 2022. Link: https://tek.io/3zrLtox

2. 25 What Is Procrastination Costing Your Business, Bitrix24 Team, 18 August 2014 Accessed 29 October 2022. Link: https://bit.ly/3zpIQ6k

Chapter 16: Twenty Time Savers

1. 25 The Best Tips To Save Time And Get Things Done. Timeular.com, August 29, 2022, Accessed 29 October 2022. Link: https://bit.ly/3WpEeau

2. Employee Time Tracking Applications Software. Capterra.com, Accessed 29 October 2022. Link: https://bit.ly/3UaTDcP

3. The Life Coach Millionaires. Life Beyond Limits, R!k Schnabel. Accessed 30 October 2022. Link: https://lifebeyondlimits.com.au/product/1632/

Chapter 17: 5x5 To Thrive Gets You Productive

1. Master Hustler' Charles Schwab Paid A Consultant A Huge Sum Of Money For Teaching His Executives This Productivity Trick. James Clear. Business Insider. 10 July 2015. Accessed 8 November 2022. Link: http://bit.ly/3DPwVAd

Chapter 19: Timely Questions

1. Have You Been Asking Yourself The Wrong Questions All Along? Salma El Shurafa. Accessed 14 November 2022. Link: http://bit.ly/3WYNxhP

Chapter 21: Guard Your Time From Thieves

1. Internet Trolls. Malavika Pradeep. Screenshot Media. 16 April 2021. Accessed 9 December 2022. Link: https://bit.ly/3FBAj3Y
2. Mercury And Health. World Health Organisation (WHO). 31 March 2017. Accessed 27 November 2022. Link: http://bit.ly/3U653hj
3. Chem Europe. Accessed 9 December 2022. Link: https://bit.ly/3Y7dhZY

4. The Actual Truth About Fluoride. Gaia. Johnny Woods. 28 March 2020. Accessed 9 December 2022. Link: https://bit.ly/3VLCfMI
5. Mental Health & Toxic Heavy Metals. Anthony William. Accessed 9 December 2022. Link: https://bit.ly/3uDrQXK

5x5 TO THRIVE

www.ingramcontent.com/pod-product-compliance
Lightning Source LLC
Chambersburg PA
CBHW020640220526
45464CB00001B/226